A REEL JOB

SHORT STORIES & THOUGHTS FROM THE RIVER

RYAN JOHNSTON

Cover image by FlamingPumpkin

Book design by Anna Burrous

ISBN 978-1-7372556-0-4

First Edition: January 2022

DEDICATION

To my bride - I'm so grateful I married my best friend. I love walking through our unique journey hand in hand with you. God has blessed us in so many ways, and my greatest blessing has been marrying you. Thank you for believing in me and supporting my dreams. I love you now and always.

To my girls - Dream BIG. You will do great things in this life. You are both so loving, smart, and beautiful. I'm so lucky to be your dad. I thank God every day that he has blessed me with you. I hope one day you can read these stories to your kids. Never forget how much I love you.

To my parents - Thank you for inspiring me to write this book. You have always been my biggest fans, always cheering me on. Thank you for showing me what loving parents are like. Your encouragement, support, and friendship have influenced me profoundly. I love you both.

To my friends - You are my second family. I am so grateful for you. Each one of you has made my life better. Thank you for being the ones I rely on for wisdom, prayer, and support. Your joy and spirit continue to impact my life.

TABLE OF CONTENTS

PROLOGUE 7

SIGHTS & SOUNDS 9

MONSTER BROWN TROUT 13

FISHING FRIENDS 19

BIG FISH MOJO 27

CRAZIES 33

DR. BANKS 39

THE PANTHER 49

THE RIVER BAR 55

SOUTHERN COMFORT 61

THE ONE FLY TOURNAMENT 69

ONE FLY LEGENDS 85

ALL NATURAL 93

EYE CANDY 101

DRY OR DIE 111

SABOTAGE 121

WHEN NATURE CALLS 127

STEAMY WEATHER 133

THE SIXTH SENSE 139

THE DARKEST OF NIGHTS 149

THE FINAL CHAPTER 161

PROLOGUE

The river is full of surprises. There are certain elements I can anticipate on any given day—the flow, the tides, the weather—but each day of guiding is a fresh story waiting to be written. Some days are normal and uneventful short stories, some are long-winded novels of struggle and victory, others are biographies of the people I encounter.

In my opinion, the true story of our lives is told through the day-to-day. We tend to focus on the large, life-changing events—and, yes, those tend to be exciting and insightful—but true life is what happens from one day to the next as we wander down life's path. The decisions we make, the things we see, the people we love, the religion we believe in, and the work we do are the things that define us.

As we look back through our careers, we can all recall moments in the workplace that made us laugh, made us angry, brought great sorrow, created joy. Through the writing of this book, I've been able to reflect on the countless river stories I've experienced. Stories of big fish caught, bigger fish lost, memorable clients, threats from wildlife encountered on the river, and just plain old funny situations shared with complete strangers. These stories you're about to read are but a taste of the sights and sounds the river has provided my clients and me over the last 20 years.

So go grab a drink and find a comfy chair. My hope is that you'll enjoy reading these tales as much as I've enjoyed living them.

SIGHTS & SOUNDS

There's something magical about floating down a river, completely immersed in an ecosystem. The sights and sounds encountered in a drift boat entertain the senses. As you listen to the noise of the bubbling river flowing over the millions of smooth cobblestone rocks, you can't help but find a brief moment in time and space where it's just you and the river. The water moves so silently and calmly in parts, then thunders violently through the rapids—one stretch of river transporting you to a meditative state while the next makes you concerned for your life. The boat is not much different than a tree that fell into the water, flowing downriver at the mercy of the current. You hear the sound of the oars gently slapping the water in some sections and then the grunts of the guide as he puts his whole might into navigating the boat through the boulder-strewn obstacle course.

Sounds of an eagle screeching in the sky above you fill your ears with nature's song as he flies across the river. The wings of the bird push so hard against the air, you can hear each flap as he tries to rise to the nest at the top of a towering dead pine tree. Then comes the noise of an osprey hitting the water behind you as it tries to catch a fish, the splash so loud it sounds like someone threw a bowling ball off the Eiffel Tower. Next, you hear the sound of the fish slapping against the osprey's talons in a desperate attempt to escape. Then, as the osprey flies away, the bird makes a shrieking noise, as if to tell the bald eagle that this morning, he has been the better fisherman.

All these sounds are enough to cause sensory overload, but when you add the dimension of actually fishing, there is never a dull moment. The sound of the reel zinging as fly line is pulled off for the first cast of the day. The faint whisper of the line dancing through the air as it effortlessly casts your fly toward the bank. The sound of a brown trout smashing your hopper is louder than a fat guy doing a belly flop. The guide yelling, "Set! Get 'em! There he is! Hit it!" so loudly that you think he's trying to yell at some other guy on the other side of the river. The whipping noise as you set the hook deep into the jaw of the trout. The stripping sound as the fly line vibrates against your fingers and rod. The noise of the line slapping your rod as the big fish swims quickly toward the middle of the river. The guide once again yelling, "Let him run! Give it line! Not so hard! Easy!" in an effort to prevent you from breaking off the fish.

Next comes the sound of the fish thrashing in the net with every last bit of energy, trying to find a way to escape. Then there is the unforgettable sound of your boatmates breaking into a celebratory roar as you've just landed that fish of a lifetime.

High fives are exchanged, everyone is laughing, compliments are shared freely, you feel like you just won Olympic gold. But the best and final sound is the one you hear as the fish swims out of the net and back to the cold depths of the river.

There are countless sounds to keep us entertained, but that's only a small part of being outdoors. The awesome beauty visible all around is enough to paint countless masterpieces. Our minds constantly snap photographs of the stunning scenery that surrounds us. Pictures of majestic, rugged mountains, tall cottonwood and pine trees soaring high above the river, and animals coming down to the water's edge for a cold, refreshing drink- they all fill our mental photo books. Each river, stream, or lake we experience creates a new album. Somewhere deep inside our brains we have a lifetime of photos, but somehow we tend to only remember the most remarkable moments.

Even small things like the aquatic bugs coming off the water are in themselves beautiful. The delicate, upright wing of a drake; the vivid color of a pale morning dun; and the dancing of a caddis on the water's surface are all pleasing to the eye. Noses of trout glisten in the sun as they rise to a mayfly hatch; they're just as breathtaking as Michelangelo's Sistine Chapel. A big trout exploding on a salmonfly brings as much excitement to a fly fisherman as watching your favorite team score a game-winning touchdown. If you are *not* a fly fisherman, you may have a hard time comprehending the beauty we find in an insect. If you are a fly fisherman, you know the joy that these petite creatures can bring to your life.

The river also provides sights and sounds that are not produced by the surrounding environment or the fishing, per se. To be honest, I think most of my best stories come from witnessing complete strangers doing unusual things on the river or its banks. These situations are not typical of a day on the water, but they tend to have long lives in my mind's eye. Memories like the couple having sex on a riverbank, the couple having sex in a raft as it floated past me, the couple sunbathing in matching black speedos while drinking Budweisers, the woman mowing her lawn in a thong bikini, intoxicated co-eds who flashed us, and numerous people and dogs falling out of boats, needing rescue.

These are the river memories that make me giggle like a schoolgirl every time I recall them. The sport of fly fishing and all of its day-to-day intricacies have influenced how I view the world, the river, and my friends. But the unpredictable events and complete strangers I've met along the way are what really make it an adventure.

Most of this book is about the lasting impressions these adventures have had on me. Some are about specific moments in time, while others are about the people I've interacted with along the way. Each one of us embarks on a potential adventure every time we leave the house. There's no telling what sights and sounds we'll encounter on any given day, or what random strangers will leave us with long-lasting memories. The beauty of going places to fly fish is taking in new sights and sounds. So get out there and explore with your fly rod in hand. Slow down and enjoy the adventure. Who knows what you'll see next? I just hope it isn't the matching speedos.

MONSTER BROWN TROUT

When you boil it down, fly fishing is a very simple sport. To have success on any given day, all you really need is a rod and reel, a handful of flies and a general idea of where to find the fish.

However, that's not to say there isn't a ridiculous amount of gear available to fly anglers, some of whom tend to go overboard with the equipment they bring to the river. This story should serve as a cautionary tale for those who think they need to outfit themselves with every gadget in the fly shop.

On this particular day, my clients were a couple of guys I have never fished with before. Mark and Brian were both in their forties, dressed casually in cargo shorts, t-shirts, ball caps, and sunglasses. My first impression was that they were a couple of family men out for a quiet day on the river, away from their kids and wives. After a quick conversation about the current conditions, flow, and weather, we decided to float a lower drift on the South Fork of the Snake River.

Upon arriving at the launch, Mark and Brian worked on getting their gear together as I prepared the boat for our float.

"Do we need any flies or leaders?" Mark asks.

"No, I always provide all the necessary gear on my fishing trips," I tell him.

"How about dry fly floatant?" he asks.

"Nope, I've got everything," I say. "To be honest, you probably should just leave your vest and net in the car."

Mark shakes his head no. "I think I'll wear it," he says. "I would feel naked and afraid without it."

I chuckle to myself as Mark pulls on his tattered tan-and-olive vest. Within its pockets he must have every fly he has collected since he was a teenager, and pinned to the pockets are countless zingers with a water thermometer, hemostats, nippers, an eyeglass cloth, and every other fly-fishing gadget known to man. He's like a clanging bell as he sways back and forth. The best part of the whole get-up is the long-handled fishing net hanging off his back.

One thing I have learned in my years of fly fishing is that I hate fishing vests. The longer you own a fly fishing vest, the more stuff you collect and the more you carry along the river. There's something to be said for being prepared for that rare size-26 pinkish-purplish-bluish trico that hatches every third generation, but I would rather not catch those fish and let my deceased great-great-grandfather down than carry around 40 pounds of fly fishing gear for eight hours.

I want to be dialed in to what's happening on the water and pack light, but I still appreciate a situation I'm not prepared for.

Let's see if I can make that trout eat a size-6 grasshopper when he's sipping tricos in the film. To me, that's fun. The fish probably doesn't eat, and great-great-grandpa rolls in his grave, but that's something I'm willing to live with if it means not having to lug around enough equipment for an entire fly-fishing club.

Mark, on the other hand, is not that kind of guy. He clearly thinks that I might not have the right bug in that extra large boat bag of mine. Or maybe he thinks I'll run out of tippet or that I don't have that battery-powered, one-handed nail knot tool from Orvis' winter catalog two years ago. I once again take a quick glance at Mark and smile at his over-stuffed vest and net. As cynical as I am, I can't help but like the guy's enthusiasm.

Mark and Brian have fished with guides several times and are familiar with the routine. Brian is sitting up front and Mark is in the back. They know how to cast, mend, and set the hook, and it isn't long before we have a nice rainbow to the net. Both guys are equally matched in their skill level. Over the next several hours we have a great time joking around, catching fish, and telling stories, but by noon it starts to get warm, with temperatures reaching the mid-90's. I notice sweat lines around Mark's vest and can tell he's starting to feel uncomfortable.

After lunch we continue our adventure down the river, but before long, Mark pipes up. "Hey, Ryan. I need to take a restroom break."

"Is it an emergency?" I ask. "Do you need to find some bushes? Or just take a leak?"

"I hate to say it, but I have to take a crap," Mark says.

"No problem," I tell him. "I'll find you a nice spot on the bank to go see if you can find Sasquatch."

I pull the boat over in a shady grove of trees. Mark gets out of the boat and goes for a walk. After 10 or 15 minutes, Brian and I start to joke that Sasquatch must have carried Mark away as a sacrifice to Quail Man (a mythical creature for another story in a different book), but Mark eventually appears from the trees with a hop in his step.

"We thought Big Foot might have gotten you," says Brian.

Mark laughs. "Hey, it's rough taking a dump in the woods," he says.

Brian and I both laugh and agree with him. I look over my shoulder and ask if Mark is ready to go. He nods yes, and we push back into the bubbling current of the river.

After a couple minutes of fishing, I start smelling a foul scent in the boat. At first, I just catch a whiff of it, but then I can't get my nose off of it. I start wondering, "Did Mark step in his own crap?" So I slowly glance over my shoulder, trying not to be suspicious, and Mark is looking at the bottom of his shoes.

"Mark, did you accidentally step in your own crap?" I ask.

"Yeah, what the hell is that smell?" says Brian.

"I don't think so," says Mark. "I can smell it too, but there's nothing on my shoes. Maybe I tracked it in when I stepped into the boat."

Mark turns around to examine the space behind him for any poop tracks. As he does, I'm faced with a huge brown turd that has landed squarely in the bottom of Mark's net. Now it's swaying back and forth as Mark looks over his shoulder.

"Holy crap, man!" I exclaim. "You crapped in your own net!"

"Mark, that is the biggest brown trout you have ever landed!" Brian cracks.

Brian and I burst into laughter as I cover my face to protect myself from the rank odor.

"I can't believe this! What do I do?" Mark asks.

"Well, the only good plan is to release that brown trout a second time," I say. "Be a true sportsman and practice catch-and-release."

So that is exactly what Mark does. He reaches up, carefully unclips his net from the D-ring on his vest, and tosses it and his brown trout into the water.

"You didn't give that brownie enough time to catch his breath before the release—or point him upstream into the current," I say between peals of laughter. "Looks like he's a floater!"

Mark chuckles with embarrassment, but before long he's laughing just as hard as Brian and me.

In all my years of fishing, that is one of the most memorable "brown trout" I have ever seen. That said, I never want to experience a brown like that in my boat ever again. If there's one thing to take from this story, it's this: Always remove your net before heading to the bushes to hunt for Sasquatch.

FISHING FRIENDS

I've met a lot of different people while fly fishing. To be honest, outside of my family, the majority of my most beloved friends have come through the sport. Whether they are clients, other guides, or random people at the fly shop, I have been blessed with amazing relationships thanks to fishing. This chapter is about the people who have dramatically changed my life and career through fly fishing. I hope one day, when I'm an old man, I can look back and reminisce about the friends I've made while chasing fins.

My introduction to fly fishing was made by my father. We had both seen the famous movie *A River Runs Through It* (or, *A River Ruined It,* as many people call it now), and all it took was Brad Pitt floating down the rapids and landing that huge, elusive brown trout to make me want to fly fish. It's funny how quickly we find out that very few people will ever have a chance to catch a fish like that.

My father, Darrel, was a fisherman from an early age but not a fly fisherman. When I was a toddler, my dad put that Snoopy rod in my hand, catching bluegill off the dock on the Colorado River in Arizona. My first real Big Fish Moment came at the age of 4 when I had a carp eat my worm under a red-and-white bobber. At that age, anything bigger than the size of my hand was a monster, and when this 10-pound carp grabbed onto my Snoopy rod, there was no chance I was letting it go. Luckily, with the help of my dad, I was hooked–by the most basic and ugly fish in the water.

As I grew older my dad kept introducing me to bigger and better things. At the age of 7, he took me on our first saltwater party boat where I caught a 20-pound sting ray. Again, not highly desirable, but at that age, it doesn't matter if you catch Nemo or a Great White; anything that bends the rod is exciting. When I started junior high school, Dad started taking me on long-range tuna boats. At the age of twelve I caught my first yellowfin, dorado, and albacore. I loved saltwater fishing. It was addicting, and who better to hang out with than my dad? But there was always something missing.

It wasn't until my twelfth birthday that I picked up a fly rod. My parents and I were on a road trip to Jackson, Wyoming, and for the big day my father purchased a guided trip for the two of us on the South Fork of the Snake River in Idaho. Now that I'm a father myself, I can see right through this generous gift. What better way to treat yourself to a little fishing than by telling the wife you're taking your son on a fly fishing trip? I have to admit, I plan to do this with my daughters someday.

On this trip, we were fortunate to book a younger guide who was willing to teach, help, and be patient with two very raw rookies. By the middle of the day, we had started to get an idea of what a cast looks like, meaning we weren't cracking off flies on our back cast every twenty minutes. This was it–I had caught the fly-fishing bug. Something about casting large dry flies to the bank and watching cutthroats slowly rise from the depths, it was addicting. From that point on, all I wanted was a fly rod in my hand.

My fly fishing passion followed a slowly sloping curve. It started with a Walmart-special five-weight that my parents bought for me. Names like Sage, Scott, and Winston didn't mean anything in my house. Manufacturers like Penn and Abu Garcia dominated our garage instead. I even remember, early in my fly fishing journey, a time when my dad was looking to buy a Penn fly reel. Now that is a very scary thought.

My first rod was a dark blue, seven-and-a-half-foot five weight that came with flies in colors of white, tan, electric blue, and black. It wasn't the prettiest of rods, but at that age I didn't know any better. It was good enough to get those dry flies in the riffle, searching for any willing nose.

After a couple years, my adolescent body outgrew the small rod, and my parents bought me a nine-foot Fenwick graphite five-weight. It was brown and not the most aesthetically pleasing rod, but it was so smooth and accurate and could cast a mile. I thought I had the Corvette of rods. I had that two-piece until I graduated high school, and it caught all kinds of fish, from trout in Wyoming to bass in California to grayling in Alaska. For me, that old Fenwick was like a blankie to a toddler. I always had it with me. There were nights I went to sleep with it close by my side. Like most rods and first wives though, it was replaced by newer, more attractive models. But I will never forget the days of casting that brown classic.

One of my best friends in school, Michael Jackson (not the famous one), along with his sister, brother, mom, and dad, all took up fly fishing at the same time. Yes, they were the Jackson Five of Fly Fishing. I was always jealous of their family. Not so much because of their name; I just thought it was so cool that they all loved the sport together. The Jackson Family went on fly fishing vacations every summer to famous rivers like the Madison, Green, San Juan, and Henry's Fork, and over time my good buddy Michael became an expert nymph fisherman.

My family was at the other end of the spectrum. We always traveled to no-name streams in the mountains, and I became an avid dry fly fisherman with an innate ability to catch little brookies and cutthroats all over the Rockies. Throwing a dry fly became a finely tuned skill of mine, but I had no idea there was so much more to fly fishing. I never knew that big fish mostly eat *under* the surface of the water.

As time went on, Michael and I started hanging out more and more and naturally started sharing stories about fish and how we caught them. Little did I know that my best friend in high school would become my Yoda, teaching me not the ways of the Force, but of the Nymph.

I know, I know…you're probably thinking that Yoda would be a guy who fishes a spey rod with traditional steelhead flies on some remote river in British Columbia. Though, come to think of it, maybe Michael was more like Darth Vader. Nymph fishermen usually do fall on the "dark side" of the Star Wars scale. However you see it, my Nymph Master would eventually teach me a skill that, over the course of my life, has paid for most of my bills. I now live in an area that is surrounded by nymph fisheries, and Michael Jackson set the foundation for my career at a very young age.

The summer we graduated high school, Michael and I with two other friends headed off to the wild Rockies for our first road trip without parents. We had planned this epic fishing trip that would take us to Colorado for 14 straight days of fishing. Over this time of chasing fins and girls and smoking my first cigar, Michael and I educated each other in our respective areas of expertise. By the end of the trip, I had become an avid nymph guy and Michael a dry fly fisherman.

In college, life began to pick up some speed. I had decided against going to a school in Oregon, Montana or Colorado for fear of turning into a fish bum, spending more time studying the water than hitting the books. So, I made what I thought was a wise decision by heading to UC Davis in Northern California. I knew by moving there, I could get out of my parents' house, do a little fishing, and maybe end up with a degree. Somehow, I didn't realize that I was moving near some of the best trout water on the West Coast. Rivers like the Sacramento, Fall, Hat Creek, Feather, and Yuba became my college playground as I spent endless hours figuring out the nuances of each. My freshman year of college, amidst meeting the girl of my dreams, I was able to fly fish more than ninety days. I managed to avoid getting kicked out of school, but there were many mornings I showed up to class with boots, gravel guards, and the smell of the river on me.

During my sophomore year, I started working in a local fly shop where I learned the ins and outs of the seasons and rivers that I had furiously fished the year before. My first real good friend in the fly-fishing world, Greg Schuerger, was the manager of a competing fly shop. Greg is the best fly fisherman I have ever met. He's the guy who patiently waits for you to flog the water with no luck, and then, with a smirk on his face, he walks in and catches five big rainbows in the exact same spot. Greg made me a better fisherman. He pushed me to wade harder, fish smaller, cast better, and be willing to go places where no one else would go. For years, Greg and I fished everywhere together, and I owe so much of my knowledge to him.

It wasn't long after working in the fly shop that I realized I could make a lot more money guiding. Nine dollars an hour working at the shop doesn't go very far, so with the help of a contribution from my grandfather, I bought a drift boat and became a guide. To this day, I'm still not sure if that was a good idea or not, but I've found a way to enjoy my life and career on the water.

When I purchased my first drift boat, I did it on a whim. I knew I wanted a boat and thought, "How hard can it be to row down a river?" My first experience rowing a boat was with my future wife. She is and always has been a gamer, willing to fly fish when most women won't. Two-day guided bonefishing trips on our honeymoon in Cozumel, then our babymoon in Hawaii. Entire summers with me in Idaho. Completing the Wyoming Cutt Slam together. Rain or shine, hot or cold or in between, she gets out there.

The first time I took her out in the boat, though, I couldn't figure out my right hand from my left as we zigged and zagged down the mighty Sacramento River. There were many times I pulled on the wrong oar, sending us spinning out of control down a fast riffle. She just laughed at me. It took me a while to get confident on the oars, but it wasn't three months before I had my first clients in the boat.

Over the years, I've made some great friends that started off as clients. If you fish with someone enough, and you enjoy being with that person, it's natural for a meaningful relationship to take hold. (Sometimes you can make enemies in the boat too.)

I have a handful of guys that I would do anything for, and it all started in my drift boat. These are the guys I now fish with on my days off, take trips with, and invite to my house for dinner. When hiring a guide, you never know if you'll spend just a day with that person or remain close with them for the rest of your life. Over time, the guide-client relationship can really deepen, becoming one of kindred spirits and fish.

In my short life, I have developed some amazing friendships, and fly fishing has often been the catalyst. There is something magical about watching a close friend land a fish of a lifetime, then replaying the memory for years afterward. I know I still have friends to meet in this life, and I have a feeling that many of them will be made through fly fishing.

BIG FISH MOJO

Ever heard of Big Fish Mojo? Do you believe in it? Do you know someone who has it? Do you have it?

Big Fish Mojo is the term used to explain why certain people always catch the biggest fish. Some might think that catching big fish requires a certain level of skill, and while aptitude doesn't hurt, it is far from requisite. Big Fish Mojo is a special gift—a blessing, really—bestowed upon a chosen few by the fish gods that always guide their fly to the biggest fish in the river or lake.

It's like the fish gods sent these people to Earth as mental ninjas just to mess with the rest of us. We get tied up in knots trying to figure out how they do it and why we can't. Many of us "others" would trade our inheritance to the fish gods for a lifetime of big catches. But the thing about Big Fish Mojo is, you don't pick it up over time. You either got it, or you don't.

My dad is the first person I ever knew with Big Fish Mojo. Of course, as a kid, I wasn't yet familiar with the phenomenon. Ever since I was little, I've watched him catch big fish. Bait fishing, fly fishing, trolling—it didn't matter. His Mojo ran high. He's won multiple jackpots on party boats, and pictures of him holding big fish have made it into the sports section of the newspaper on at least two separate occasions. As a naive kid, I thought my dad must have been a super-human fisherman compared to all the other anglers out there. But now I know better (sorry, Dad). He's just an average guy with some basic skills. He knows what he's doing in most circumstances, but he isn't an expert by any means. When he goes fishing, crowds don't exactly gather to behold his prowess. So, how to explain the giant catches? Clearly, he's in the Big Fish Mojo Club. He's been given the magical gift of finding—and catching—ridiculously large fish.

I've put a lot of time in since my Snoopy rod days, and after 25 years of fly fishing, I consider myself rather skilled at it. I don't mean to brag on my fishing skills, but some context might lend a bit of perspective to my father's paranormal fishing abilities. I have been guiding for trout and steelhead for almost two decades and have become quite proficient in fishing for both species. I can walk out into a river in various situations and catch lots of trout. I can go steelheading on most West Coast rivers and expect to catch a handful of chromers. This is what I do for a living, after all, and over time we just get better, right?

I'm still working on my saltwater game, but even so, my casting ability has given me a leg up on my dad. The two of us have been fly fishing together for nearly 30 years and he still can't figure out a double haul, even though I've tried to teach him a dozen times. He'll get there.

Dad and I have taken lots of fly fishing trips together: red fishing in Texas, bone fishing in Hawaii, trout fishing in Wyoming and Idaho, steelheading in Northern California, and blue-water fishing off of San Diego. Then there are the quick trips to local ponds, creeks, and rivers. Every one of them was awesome because I was fishing with my dad. He has literally been my best fishing buddy since, well, Snoopy. On most trips I out-fish my dad two or three to one. If my dad catches 5 trout, I've landed 10 to 15. If he hooks 3 steelhead, odds are I'll hook 6. My dad always catches a decent handful, but I consistently put the beat down on him in terms of sheer numbers.

And yet somehow, on every trip, he always manages to find the big one. It doesn't matter if we're fishing freshwater or saltwater, his Mojo pulls the big fish in. I don't get it. How can someone get out-fished over and over and always catch the biggest fish? The law of averages suggests I should catch the biggest fish from time to time, right? But then, math and logic don't apply to fishing. The fish gods give the Mojo, and they don't give a damn about our rules or logic.

Another angler with some serious Big Fish Mojo is my buddy Steve. I helped Steve learn how to fly fish; our friendship started with him as a client in my boat. Actually, the first time Steve stepped into my boat, he was pretty much a rookie. After a couple years, he became a very proficient fly fisherman. We've fished quite a bit on trout and steelhead rivers in Northern California, and it didn't take long before I started to notice his supernatural Mojo.

The first trip Steve ever took with me was on the Lower Sacramento River in the fall. He hooked three steelhead that day in a place where you're lucky to find just one. On our second trip, in spring when there's only a handful of steelhead in the Lower Sac, Steve still somehow found a five-pound chromer. Steve's third trip with me was in the middle of summer when there are *no* steelhead in the system. I mean zilch. Somehow this guy manages to find a big wild steelhead. Ridiculous. This went on for several years. I'd go months without a client landing a steelhead, then Steve shows up and magically pulls one out. Before long he was given a proper nickname: Steelhead Steve.

My other clients grew jealous, maybe even a little suspicious, of Steelhead Steve's big fish pictures on my website. Occasionally one would ask if I'd fished with Steelhead Steve recently and if he'd caught any big fish. He kind of became something of a legend among them. Steve, of course, loved the nickname and the reputation.

Then one April, on the Lower Sac again, Steve and I are trout fishing a famous riffle that's generally full of rainbows. Every once in a while you *might* find a couple steelhead there. All of a sudden, Steve's indicator violently shoots under the water. He sets the hook like a mad man and this big fish rolls right under the surface. It turns, throws a huge spray of foamy, white water off its tail fin, and rips off downstream taking over a hundred feet of backing with it.

"Steelhead Steve does it again!" I say in an excited voice. "I haven't caught a steelhead since November, and you find one in April!"

I row straight downriver, and the fish decides to stay in the deep, using its weight to prolong the fight.

After several minutes, Steve asks, "How big do you think it looked?"

"Probably eight pounds," I tell him.

As the fight continues, I start to get glimpses of Steve's steelhead. Something looks a little funny. It's much more olive-colored than usual.

"Uh, I don't think you have a steelhead on your line, man," I tell Steve.

He disagrees. "It's fighting like a steelhead," he says.

"Well, of all people, you should know," I say. "It made a hard move, had a long run, and then started to sulk on the bottom. That screams steelhead, for sure. But something just isn't right. Not enough silver and white to make me believe this thing is a chromer."

After a couple more minutes of fighting, the fish is getting tired. Finally, up from the depths of the river comes... a 28-inch... *squawfish?!?* (If you're unfamiliar with the squawfish, or northern pikeminnow, it's considered a trash fish, in the same category as carp, suckers, whitefish, or mullet.) I am stunned. I've never seen a squawfish this big. It's literally the Squawfish of a Lifetime.

Steve, on the other hand, is confused. And disappointed. But man, I am excited about this fish!

"We've gotta take a picture with this thing, man," I tell Steve. "This is a true trash-fish trophy!"

And in that glorious moment, Steve's nickname quickly changed from Steelhead Steve to Squawfish Steve, to our great pleasure and entertainment.

These days, Squawfish Steve still catches more than his share of big steelhead—the Mojo doesn't leave, after all—but never a fish quite as memorable as that monstrous pikeminnow.

You can decide for yourself if Big Fish Mojo is real or not. Maybe it's like believing in aliens or Bigfoot—only the true believers ever seem to witness it. All I know is I do believe, one hundred percent. I have personally seen the Big Fish Mojo in action with my very own eyes. My dad and Squawfish Steve are only two of many. There are plenty of anglers out there with the same paranormal gift.

If you are one of those chosen few, well, good for you. Maybe keep it to yourself, though. And understand this: It is not to your credit. A gift has been bestowed upon you. Use it with caution. If over exerted, it can lead to an inflated ego, a fishing addiction, or worst of all, alienation from and sabotage by jealous fishing buddies. Check those shared flies for weakened hooks, you know what I mean? What can I say, we all want to be the hero, and most will stop at nothing to catch the biggest fish.

CRAZIES

Fly fishermen are crazy. Well, maybe I should be more specific. Fly fishing *makes* people crazy, primarily because there's a considerable amount of competition involved in this sport. We race each other to the prime spots, try to out-smart whatever elusive fish we're chasing, attempt to out-fish our buddies, and we're secretive about how many fish we caught or what fly we used. When we're asked, "How was the fishing?" our responses are intentionally vague.

"It was slow."

"We got a handful."

"It was okay."

Each of us wears a mask of sorts and refuses to ever divulge the complete truth. Whether that lack of truth stems from embarrassment for spending an entire day on the river and not hooking a single fish, or having hooked a fish on every cast, or having found a hot new fly that out-fished all the other go-to patterns in the local fly shop, or simply because we want to be the one who catches more fish than anyone else, it all comes from a competitive root that's buried deep and tangled into most fishermen's souls.

Fly fishing causes us to generally dislike other anglers. Once we get on the water and find our spot, we become like the seagulls in the Disney movie *Nemo*: "Mine! Mine! Mine! Mine!" For the briefest moment in time, that little piece of river real estate becomes ours. We will do anything to protect our small, beautiful river kingdom. Thoughts like, *"This is my riffle," "I can't believe another guy walked in below me," "I hate jet boats," "I hate any type of boat," "I can't believe this guy thinks there is enough space for both of us to fish this run," "I hate nymph fishermen,"* and *"I hate everyone else on this river,"* run through our minds. This competitive desire to conquer the river, the fish, and the other fishermen overtakes our good sense and makes us do crazy things.

Fishing can turn the most level-headed person into a possessive, angry, aggressive river creature. Every fisherman has experienced, or at some point will experience, the "Angry Fly Fisherman." When you do, be aware that things may get ugly fast. Over the years, multiple anglers have cussed me out on the river. Some have even offered to fight me right on the spot. Twice, wade fishermen have thrown rocks at my clients and me. Another time, a guide hammered a huge nail into the sidewall of my tire. I once heard about a guy stealing another angler's boat plugs while he was doing a shuttle. My friends have had lug nuts taken off their wheels. Another had all his windows shot out with a rifle. All in the name of catching a fish.

Sometimes fly fishermen quickly, and without warning, turn into apes, beating their chests in an effort to prove who is the Alpha Silverback of the river. Of all the crazy things I've seen, one fall day on the Feather River will forever stay in my memory bank.

It was a normal, busy day of steelhead fishing on the Feather, but working around other boats and wade fishermen, my clients and I were able to find plenty of willing fish. The weather was beautiful, the steelhead were biting, and I had some of my favorite clients in the boat—the kind of day guides dream about. Later in the afternoon, we were floating toward one of the best and most popular riffles in the entire river. When guiding, I never plan on fishing this hundred yard stretch, since there are usually two or three wade fishermen already camped there, and this day was no different. There was one wade fisherman at the top of the run and a second at the bottom.

When it comes to good boat etiquette, the rule of thumb is to float behind wade fishermen when possible, and that was my plan with the guy at the top of the riffle. I could see he was wearing high-end Simms waders and using a switch rod—standard issue for most steelheaders on the Feather. He didn't acknowledge us as we approached, but once we were about 50 feet away, with his stare still fixed on the water, he growled loudly , "This is my hole!"

My clients and I exchanged "What did he say?" glances.

"Hey, buddy, what did you say?" I asked in a clear voice.

"Don't talk to me!" he responded.

"Okay. I'm just gonna float behind you and get out of your way," I assured him.

"I said, don't talk to me," he quickly fired back.

"Okay. We'll be outta here in a couple seconds," I reply.

The fisherman then yelled at the top of his lungs, "Don't come at me like that!"

"I'm not coming at you, just floating by," I told him.

"Stop coming at me. This is my hole. You want to fight? Don't come at me like that!" The words were rapidly firing out of his mouth.

Suddenly, he started charging the boat aggressively through calf-deep water like a caveman.

"Let's go! Let's fight right here!" he yelled.

My two clients and I stood up. We were ready to defend ourselves against this maniac. He charged faster and harder. I quickly lifted my oar in protection. It hit the middle of his chest. He powerfully slapped it out of the way, looking surprised. This stymied his attack long enough for the speed of the river to take us past him. He was cussing us out as soon as we were out of reach. Then quickly he charged back toward the bank.

Once he got about five feet from land, he tossed his fly rod into the bushes and ran down the gravely bank in full sprint. The way he traversed that bank in his waders, he was so agile—it was impressive. As we entered the middle part of the riffle, where there were no anglers, I told my clients to ignore the lunatic for just a minute and make a cast off the right side of the boat. The two of them gathered themselves and made a pair of good casts directly into the bucket of the riffle.

Within seconds, the client in the back of the boat hooked a chrome-bright, pissed-off eight-pound steelhead. The fish proceeded to cartwheel down the river, ripping off fly line faster than a bank robber leaving the scene of the crime. Jump after jump revealed a beautiful steelhead throwing herself in every direction, trying to spit the hook.

As this picturesque situation played out, all we heard in the background was one F bomb after another. I looked over my shoulder to see the crazy man jumping over dead branches and rocks as he tried to keep up with us. Deep down inside I felt a sense of competitive pride knowing that he probably spent hours looking for that fish, and it was a couple hundred feet downstream of him now.

Some would say I'm the crazy one for fishing the riffle when there was a "river monster" chasing us downstream. Well, it's like I said: Anything for a fish.

We fought the steelhead for three or four minutes with a serenade of expletives coming from our friend on the bank. Once we landed and released the fish, we immediately turned our attention back to him. As we did, he yelled, "I was in the war for twenty-three years. I'm gonna get my gun. You better watch your back. One of these days I'm gonna get you when you never expect it!"

As soon as we heard the word "gun," I quickly started to row down the river, trying to put a greater distance between us. As we floated farther and farther away, he continued to yell obscenities. Every couple seconds, one of us would look back to keep an eye on him.

Then, suddenly, there was dead silence.

"Where did he go?" I asked.

There was no sign of him on the bank, no bushes moving, no more yelling, no walking back to his rod, nothing. He had vanished in an instant. It was extremely eerie and uncomfortable, and the first time I ever felt fear on the river. We all had visions of this guy holding his rifle, looking through his scope, hunting us down. I had been involved in yelling matches on the river and had experienced lots of pissed-off anglers, but nothing had ever been this intense and threatening.

For the rest of the day, we nervously scanned the banks for the enraged angler. We agreed that he was either on drugs, mentally ill, or a combination of the two. How incredibly it went from 0 to 100 in a matter of seconds.

This guy snapped, but what did he snap over? A sport that most of us do for relaxation, to become one with the river, to have fun, to escape our daily stresses in life... A small part of me is still afraid to run into that guy again. What if, next time, he takes it to another level, and actually reveals a firearm?

I'll be the first to admit that fishing can make us all a little crazy. A competitive nature will cause the calmest of anglers to lose control of their emotions from time to time. And sometimes, the voices in our heads convince us that there's not enough space for other people. But the beauty of fishing is there are always other spots and other fish to be caught. If you ever encounter an angler who reminds you of Gollum from *Lord of the Rings*, slowly petting his gold Abel reel and muttering "My precious," consider letting him have the spot. Find one of your own.

DR. BANKS

The alarm on my phone breaks the silence of the morning, awakening me from a peaceful slumber. I miss the button with my first blind swing but connect with the second, then stumble down the stairs feeling the brisk spring air against my body.

I dress for the day, hop into my truck, and head down the road, the start of an hour-long drive to meet my client at the boat launch. I turn on the radio and start listening to the latest sports news. After about ten minutes of *blah, blah, blah,* my thoughts drift to fish caught, missed, and broke off on trips earlier in the week. I start playing out the day ahead in my mind.

Each morning, I lose myself in imagining what today will be like and what fishing strategy will be necessary. It's like a game of chess as I envision moving the pawns forward, then strategically moving the bishop, ready to strike. Next I attack with the size 16 Prince Nymph as one by one, check mate to each trout that enters the net.

In my idealism, I envision cutthroat noses rising to big Western Green Drakes over and over. Or big, bright coastal steelhead rolling in my favorite hole. Or fishing egg patterns to extra large rainbows behind stacks of spawning salmon. This kind of optimism is what keeps us fly fishermen alive and kicking. We just know that around every corner there's a chance for the most epic fishing of our lives. The reality is, it usually doesn't happen that way, but it doesn't hurt to dream. After losing myself in my "Alice and Troutland" moment for most of the drive, I gain my senses as I pull up to the boat launch and find my client, Jack, leaning against his car, rod strung up and ready to go.

I hop out of my truck and walk over to introduce myself. Jack's a nice-looking, middle-aged gentleman in his 40s, wearing khaki shorts, a green plaid vented Patagonia shirt, and flip flops. We chit chat for a few minutes; I find out Jack is a surgeon from San Francisco and a veteran fly angler.

"Jackpot!" I think to myself. "A client who potentially has a decent amount of disposable income and enjoys fly fishing." The idealist in me is already booking Jack for additional trout and steelhead trips in the fall.

I put the boat in the water, and I'm rigging up Jack's rod with the appropriate leader, flies, and split shot, when I ask him one of the first questions I always ask a new client: "When's the last time you fished?" My perfect vision of this epic trout day hangs delicately in the balance as I await Jack's answer. If he responds with "last summer," then we have some hope. If the answer is "last month," I'll be as giddy as a kid who just hit his first homerun. However, if the response is something like "five years ago," I know I can kiss my dreams of a perfect day goodbye.

"Just two weeks ago," Jack says.

"Cha-ching!" I think to myself.

I ask where he went on his last trip.

"I went to Utah, to the Flaming Gorge on the Green River, to fish the blue wing olive hatch," he replies.

Sweet! Not only am I guiding someone who fishes on a regular basis, but most fly fishermen don't go to a potentially snowy Flaming Gorge in April to catch fish on small mayflies unless they have some serious interest. By now, I am extremely excited for what the day holds.

Jack then mentions other rivers he's fished. Famous, big-name rivers like the Henry's Fork, Madison, Big Horn, South Platte, and San Juan make the list. We talk of places where we've both fished and compare notes on our experiences. At this point, a definite sense of camaraderie is starting to build, and we haven't even cast a line yet.

"Have you ever fished the Lower Sacramento before?" I ask.

"No, but I've always wanted to, since it's only three hours from home," he says. "It's much easier to get in the car and drive a few hours than it is to fly to the Rockies to fish."

"You're going to love it," I tell him. "But you should know we do things a little differently on this river compared to most trout streams."

As I explain to Jack, the Lower Sacramento River is a big western tailwater that flows between 3,000 and 15,000 cubic feet per second depending on the demand for water from farmers. The river is fairly deep and has a significant gradient that gets the water running and tumbling downstream. Bug life on the river mainly consists of caddis and mayflies; there are very few stoneflies and terrestrials. Most of the trout's main food source floats down the heavy current in the middle of the river. Therefore, most of the trout live on the edges of the main current line, looking for bugs to feast upon. As I explain all of this to Jack, he listens intently and nods his head in understanding and contemplation.

"Yeah, that does sound different than most fly fishing I've done," he says. "But I'm excited about the potential of hooking into big rainbows so close to home. So, whatever you wannna do, I'm game for it. I'm just here to catch fish, hang out, and have a good time."

"This is gonna be a fun day," I think to myself.

We finally start fishing, and after a handful of casts it becomes very apparent that Jack is an experienced fly fisherman. Everything he does—the speed and accuracy of the casts, his mending, his ability to read the water—is flawless. Within five minutes Jack is hooked up on his first rainbow. As I watch him fight the fish, I can tell he's focused, confident, and excited all at the same time—the demeanor you'd expect from a fly fishing surgeon. After a short battle, a brilliant 18-inch rainbow with deep pink and crimson stripes running down its side comes to the net.

"That was great," Jack says as he gives me a quick high five. "Good job, guide. That's a good way to start the day."

Within the next thirty minutes, Jack lands three more rainbows all in the same size class. My epic "Alice and Troutland" day has started out nicely, though as we go around the next bend the fishing starts to slow up. We've come to a small section of river where we're out of the good runs, and my plan is to fish through the unproductive water quickly in order to get to the next good spot.

"Look at that bank on the other side of the river," Jack says as we drift along.

I look over and notice a very fishy-looking bank that would certainly hold trout in most rivers.

"Let's give that bank a try," he says.

I quickly remind him that the majority of trout on the Lower Sac like to live in the middle of the river, as there is very little insect life on the bank.

"Oh, yeah, that's right" he responds. After this brief conversation we get back to the fishing, and it isn't long before Jack is hooked up again. This time he lands a big, fat, healthy 22-inch rainbow.

"Wow! I pay a lot of money each year trying to catch a fish like that in Montana," says Jack. "I never knew I only had to drive a few hours to have this experience."

At this point in the trip, I'm really starting to have fun. Jack is a nice guy and a great fly fisherman, the fishing is good, and the sun is out. What more can I ask for?

After a couple more trout to the net, we hit another slow period that lasts about forty-five minutes. Near the end of this catch-less stretch, Jack says, "Check out those seams coming off the logs on the bank."

Once again, I look over to the bank and see a very "trouty" looking spot. Jack is correct in his thinking, but he's on the wrong river for that technique to work.

"Yeah, that looks like a good spot, but there aren't going to be any fish over there," I tell him. "You need to trust me on this one. I know that you want to fish the banks, but you have to let the river dictate where you fish."

Jack nods his head in agreement as he closely watches his indicator float down the deep seam line against the main current. By the time we break for lunch, Jack has landed a dozen trout and lost a handful more—an incredibly solid start to the day. As we eat our lunch, we continue to have good conversation about families, work and fishing. After twenty minutes of sitting in the shade to rest, Jack decides he's ready for more. He was not joking when he said he was here to catch fish.

Right after lunch we hit a flurry of trout off a major shelf in the middle of the river. Six strong, healthy rainbows come to the net one by one. Jack is getting pumped at this point. Not much is better for an angler than pulling on fish for 30 minutes straight.

As we continue down the river, we once again hit some unproductive spots and the fishing slows again. After about ten minutes of not catching anything, Jack's eyes start to wander to the banks. I notice he is only partially watching his indicator at this point. He studies every logjam, every section of over-hanging grass, every bit of riprap along the bank…

"Let's go fish that seam coming off that big cottonwood on the bank," he says, predictably.

"Jack, there are no fish over there," I tell him.

"C'mon, let's go try it. It's too good-looking not to have a trout sitting behind it, waiting to inhale my Prince Nymph," he responds.

At this point, it's evident that he absolutely, one-hundred-percent believes there are fish living on the banks. Clearly the eighteen trout he's already landed near the middle of the river mean nothing—he *really* wants to fish that seam line.

After a brief internal battle, I decide that it's best for all of us if Jack gets to fish the bank. I row across the river and set Jack up for the perfect drift behind the drowned cottonwood.

As his flies hit the water, I can sense that Jack is anticipating a strike right away. His back gets rigid and his hand tightens slightly on the cork of his rod—the classic look of someone who believes a bite is imminent. It doesn't take long for that hand to loosen and his head to start looking back upriver at his perfect trout spot. Jack didn't catch a fish on that log, and the disappointment was all over his face—like a kid opening the cookie jar to find only crumbs from yesterday. Jack's eyes start to scan again.

"Hey, look at that big rock against the opposite bank," he says.

I tell him for the fourth time that we need to fish the middle of the river. "The big rock looks really good," I say, "but just like with the log back there, we're not gonna catch anything."

"C'mon, give it one more try," he says.

I begrudgingly row to the other side of the river.

As we approach the big boulder, he makes a flawless cast. Jack is probably a better fisherman than half the guides on the river, and every move he makes for fifty yards behind this rock is done with precision. *Cast, mend. Cast, mend. Cast, mend.*

"Come on, fish, eat it!" he yells.

But, like the perfect log jam, the perfect boulder does not produce a fish. Again, the look of defeat comes upon him, and this time I can see the Lower Sac is starting to mess with his head. He looks downriver, upriver, and out to the middle. Then, with his shoulders slightly slumped, he says, "Let's try that next bank."

I look up at Jack with a puzzled look. "What's the goal of this trip?" I ask him. "To catch fish or to try fishy-looking spots?"

"The goal from the start was to catch as many fish as possible," he replies.

"Then we need to go back to fishing the middle of the river and stop trying to fish the Lower Sac like it's the Madison," I tell him. "Your instinct is right—the banks look good—but like I said all day, there are no fish there. If you want to be successful, let the expert on the river help you achieve your goals."

Jack doesn't take to that comment very well. His body gets rigid again. This time it isn't because of the fishing.

"You are the worst f***ing fly fishing guide I have ever hired," he snarls at me.

Alrighty then. We are officially through the looking glass. This guy has just snapped. Clearly there's something more to it than what I just said to him, so I respond as nicely as I can.

"That's your opinion, and I respect that. But what I said was not meant to disrespect you—only to help you catch more fish."

"You are a f**king idiot," he replied.

"If you're not having fun here, then we can go home," I tell him.

"Yeah, row my ass home."

"Okay, no problem."

The final five miles of our drift takes about an hour. Not a word is spoken. The sound of my oars dipping in and out of the rushing water is the only sound breaking the awkward silence. I keep biting my tongue as every cuss word in the book comes to mind. I want to scream at Jack, but I know that nothing good can come from a yelling match in a small boat. The last thing I want is to make this confrontation worse. So I focus my energy into my oars, trying to stroke harder and faster to get Dr. Jackass off my boat as quickly as possible.

After what seems like an eternity, we finally get to the take-out spot. As soon as the boat hits solid ground, Jack gets out and quietly walks to the top of the hill. He doesn't look at me or speak a single word. A deep, serious, angry look on his face is all that reveals how he's feeling.

I follow him up with some of my gear, then I back the truck down to the boat. Once it's secure on the trailer, I drive up the hill to load the rest of my gear, then hop back into the driver's seat. Jack's been breaking down his rod, but now he walks over to my passenger door, so I roll down the window.

"What are you doing?" I ask.

"Well, you have to take me back to my car," he says.

"When you call me a f**king idiot, you don't get a ride back to your car," I tell him.

As Jack's jaw drops, I put my foot on the gas pedal. I'm watching him in the rearview mirror as I drive away. All I can see is an angry surgeon from San Francisco, with one hand in the air, showing me I was his "Number 1" guide.

I don't know what happened to Jack. I suppose he ended up calling a cab. To be honest, I don't really care. Maybe next time he'll think twice about being a jerk to his fly fishing guide.

THE PANTHER

They say the clothes make the man, but I can tell you they don't always make the fisherman. One day, I walked into the fly shop to meet my clients Matt and Travis and found two guys dressed for an official board meeting with the fish. You know the look: collared guide shirts, khaki shorts, wading sandals, and hats that are crisp and clean from their most recent summer fishing destination, usually some high-end lodge on the Madison, San Juan, or North Platte. Everything carefully curated to give the impression of an experienced fly fisherman. While this look might fool acquaintances into thinking the person sporting it is an expert angler, it's usually a red flag for guides.

Nonetheless, after introductions, my clients and I start talking about where we should fish for the day and decide to try one of the lower drifts on the South Fork of the Snake River.

We load up my truck and boat and head down the highway through Swan Valley. For the next 30 minutes, we talk of places fished, big fish missed and caught, the current fishing conditions, the weather—anything of interest to pass the time before we really find out if these guys' casting and fishing skills match their clothing.

We eventually make our way to the boat launch where we'll start our drift. I hop out of the truck and start getting the boat ready for the day. While I'm running around putting the anchor on, loading the boat with extra rods and my gear bag, unstrapping the boat, and making sure everything is in place for these fine gentlemen, they're getting their rods ready.

Once the rods are strung, I take over and start rigging the flies I've chosen for the day—a tan Chernobyl Ant with a Lightning Bug dropper, a combo that has worked for the previous 30 days at fooling dumb cutthroats and the odd brown trout here and there. Once I get the two fly rods rigged, I'm surprised when one of them hands me...a spinning rod? Like most people, I got my start in trout fishing using spinning gear, but age and wisdom have shown me that fly fishing is the far superior method.

"What is this rod for?" I ask, somewhat incredulously.

"It's in case the fish don't eat flies today," Travis replies.

"The fish are gonna eat these flies just fine," I tell him. "They have been all over this combination the past month. Besides, cutthroats aren't really picky."

Travis insists on bringing the rod just in case, so I stash it in the boat where no one can see it.

We eventually get the boat launched and begin our float down the mighty Snake. To start the day, we cast toward grassy undercut banks—the most ideal western dry fly fishing one can imagine. Long, tall grass hanging over a mud bank, with lots of salmon flies and golden stones falling into the water, creates a great home for hungry and willing trout. It doesn't take long to see that these guys are quite accomplished casters. Fishing down the first bank results in several nice trout to the net and many more aggressive strikes missed. At this point I'm thinking, "What's the reason for the spinning rod?"

For the next several hours, we rise fish after fish. Everyone is having a great time. It's the kind of morning that makes a guide feel like a god...until he remembers it's not his skill that's bringing success, but rather being in the middle of a huge stonefly hatch with bugs the size of small birds flying around everywhere. Regardless, if this keeps up, my clients will have an epic day of catching fish.

I decide to stop for lunch on a beautiful riffle coming off a gravel bar, knowing it won't be long until the pale morning duns start to hatch. This will be the perfect situation: fish rising to small mayflies in the riffles and huge stoneflies on the bank. As we start eating lunch, I see a nose come up and sip the first PMD of the day. By the time we're done eating, there are at least 20 trout eating PMDs in this riffle. It's a beautiful scene, as noses glisten in the sun, trying to suck in every bug possible. The fish look like little sharks gorging themselves, with rises of nose-fin, nose-fin, nose-fin. I decide to tie on two small PMD emerger patterns that sit slightly in the surface film. Travis, smiling ear to ear like a boy just kissed for the first time, steps up to take the first cast.

It lands beautifully in front of a cutthroat, right in the path of destruction, and almost immediately gets eaten. I start yelling

"Set! Set!" but nothing happens. No rod movement. No attempt to set the hook.

"Okay, just take another shot," I say.

Travis's second cast is just as good as the first one, and—*boom*—another fish comes up and eats. "Set! SET!" Again nothing.

"Are you having a hard time seeing your fly?" I ask.

"Yeah, I can't see it," he says.

"That's okay," I tell him. "When I say 'set,' raise your rod just like you were fishing down the banks."

However, the third and fourth casts produce the same result.

"I know you're having a hard time seeing the fly, but I need you to trust me that the fish are eating it," I say.

Then Travis starts to reveal his dark spin-fisherman side.

"I don't believe that the fish are eating the fly," he says.

"What?" I respond. "Why would I make up a story? I want you to be successful and hook these fish."

"I don't believe you," he repeats.

"Well, I can show you I'm not lying if you let me have a cast," I say.

I hook a fish with my first cast.

"That was luck," he says. "Let's see you do it again."

At this point, I'm shaking my head in disbelief, but I happily take another shot to prove my client wrong. I cast and get the same result. I can sense the frustration level rising in the boat.

"No way you can do that a third time," he says.

With my next cast, I aim at the biggest fish in the riffle, and a long, beautiful brown snout comes up to take a taste of the little morsel. I set the hook and bring the 22-inch brown trout to the net.

"Nope, those fish were definitely not eating that fly," I say sarcastically.

After my three "lucky" casts, Travis decides to take another swing at it. He actually sets the hook on the first cast, but he's late. He whiffs on his second cast and the third cast comes up empty on a wicked eat. I should've pulled my anchor and gone back to throwing big dry flies down the banks, but I was reluctant to leave with so many fish rising in the riffle.

"This is bullshit," Travis says. "Hand me my spinning pole and get a black-and-yellow Panther Martin out of my vest."

No. No. No. I can't believe this is happening. I tell Travis that the Panther Martin is not going to work since the fish are dialed in to small PMDs and won't like a big, flashy spinner. Of course, he has different ideas and insists I set up his pole, which I reluctantly do. Now I know for sure this guy missed out on Fly Fishing 101. Maybe the fancy apparel didn't come with instructions. Travis takes his pole and makes cast after cast with the Panther Martin. After about 20 minutes of flogging the water, he decides to change to a different color—yellow with red dots. Needless to say, he did not get a different result.

After beating the water over and over, he finally gives up. I decide to try and salvage the trip by going back to fishing the banks with the larger flies. We spend the rest of the day recovering from the lost PMD battle, but end up winning the war by catching lots of great browns and cutthroats off the banks with big stoneflies.

On my drive home that day, I realize that while the clothes sometimes do send a message, more often than not, a spinning pole is a worse sign than the Gucci fly fishing clothes. We can try to fool our peers by dressing the part, but only the fish can validate our skill.

THE RIVER BAR

Beer and fly fishing go well together. Whiskey and fly fishing go well together. Vodka and fly fishing go well together. Actually, I'm not sure if there's a type of alcohol that doesn't go well with fly fishing.

Well, maybe not a wine spritzer. But then again, I'm sure there's some beautiful, amazing woman fly fisher who loves a little spritzer break on the riverbank. Now, if you're a male and you enjoy a little spritzer while throwing dry flies on the Madison River, then I may have to question your "Man Card." See, alcohol and fishing are made for each other. Alcohol makes a lot of things more entertaining and enjoyable. Weddings, karaoke, 2-year-olds' birthday parties—all are perfectly fine on their own, but each is greatly enhanced with the addition of booze. Alcohol, when used in moderation, makes things—fly fishing included—better.

Personally, I'm a beer guy on the river. Sitting in the boat, drinking a cold one while a buddy casts a dry fly to a pod of rising cutthroats, it brings me to a deep peace. In that moment, the whole world seems to connect on a deeper level. The river is flowing, the fly is dancing on the water, and the beer is sharpening the senses. Now, could the same moment happen without alcohol? Of course. But for me, a cold microbrew is the final piece of the puzzle. Over the years, I have enjoyed some great moments with my friends Sierra Nevada, Big Sky Brewing, Lagunitas, Bear Republic, Russian River Brewing, to name a handful. These are the friends that have never let me down—they always leave a smile on my face at the end of the day.

Now, you noticed I did NOT mention beers like Budweiser, Coors, Pabst Blue Ribbon, or Natty Light. See, to be a true fly fisherman, the first rule of thumb is this: You need to drink specialty microbrews. The more you start paying attention to the fly fishing community, the more you will notice that the majority of fly fisherman tend to be beer snobs. I must include myself in this category. If I'm drinking a beer, I want it to have some flavor, some depth to the taste, to be refreshing, and to be something that is just plain good to drink. There's nothing wrong with the major beer brands, but they just don't do it for me. I personally want to drink something that has some body and doesn't feel like I'm drinking glorified water.

Now, if you're into red-and-white bobber fishing or have a little bell on the end of your rod, then Budweiser or Coors is probably the beer for you. There's something about a Styrofoam cup full of worms that just screams "CHEAP BEER." If the Silver Bullet or a Bud Light Lime—aka "Sprite Beer"—is the only thing available, I have been known to partake in the dark side. But deep down, when drinking these beers, I can feel my soul being shaken. Microbrews, in my opinion, are just plain better. Not to mention, something about the taste bud experience matches the aura of the fly fishing lifestyle.

Some would say that wine is more befitting to the sport of fly fishing. I'll admit that a glass of Malbec after a day of casting to sea-run browns in Argentina, or a nice Pinot Noir at the end of a long day of steelheading in Northern California, makes a lot of sense. But I maintain that wine doesn't belong on the river. Who has enough space for a wine bottle opener in their vest anyway? I already have too much stuff in my vest and that opener might be enough to break open the zippers. Plus, if I'm putting anything extra into my vest, it will be those size-36 midges I may need one day to match the midge hatch that only comes off when all of the planets in our solar system align.

Some guides and lodges provide a streamside meal complete with wine, white tablecloth, candlelight, and a violin player, but most fly fishermen I know are on the river to fish. Lunch is just fuel to get us through the afternoon. I'll opt for a beer to wash down my soggy turkey sandwich and salty chips over a bottle of wine any day.

I typically don't drink hard liquor on the river. I do enjoy a good cocktail while sitting by the fire recounting my day on the water. That said, the hard stuff is the tipple of choice for many anglers while fishing. Most frequently, fly fishermen who like to drink liquor on the river tuck their trusty flask into their vest or jacket pocket. There's nothing like taking a pull of whiskey on a cold winter steelhead stream. It not only gives you a burst of energy, but it momentarily warms your body from the inside out, as if a pointy-eared Christmas elf has started a nice, warming fire deep in your belly. For that moment you forget that you are freezing your ass off trying to catch a stupid fish.

I have lots of clients who bring a flask with them on their trips. Sometimes the flasks are the size of a small wallet and other times they're large enough to accommodate a Big Gulp. I'll never forget the time a younger client showed up with a CamelBak—basically a soft-sided flask that you carry on your back—full of rum and Coke. I was impressed by the ingenuity, and it confirmed for me that fly fishermen will go to great lengths to have their favorite alcoholic beverage on the river. I have had clients bring battery-operated blenders to make margaritas; mix complex Bloody Mary's with fresh-cut limes, celery, and pickled asparagus; and, yes, even go so far as to pair a wine with the turkey sandwich for lunch.

One of the more entertaining—yet potentially problematic—aspects of combining drinking and fly fishing is when clients start making up drinking games on the river. Just like college students playing beer pong, flip cup, and kings cup, older, well-to-do professional types can sometimes lose themselves in the river world. While steelhead fishing, I had one group of guys take a shot every time someone in the boat hooked a fish. For their sake and mine, we only hooked five fish that day. They were well spread out.

Another twosome decided to take a hit off the flask every time they had a "double" while trout fishing on the Lower Sac. A "double" means that, at the same time, both anglers are hooked up on fish. This particular day was the opposite of the steelhead trip; we had six doubles by eleven o'clock that morning. As the day went on, the fishing kept getting better, and their buzzes eventually turned into full-on inebriation.

I started skipping the good holes, knowing that my clients needed a break from the hooch.

Over the years, I've seen lots of guys and gals enjoy a drink in my boat. More often than not, that's an occasional cold beer on a hot summer day or a nip of whiskey to warm the cockles. The issue is when drinking becomes the focus and the fishing becomes secondary. Just like anything in life, alcohol requires moderation. I once had a couple of clients bring a 30-pack of Coors Light and a bottle of Jack Daniels– for the two of them. They started drinking as I was rigging up their rods at seven o'clock in the morning, and by noon there was no alcohol left in the boat. See, these two guys were there to drink, not to fly fish.

This extreme circumstance is when fly fishing and alcohol are not good for each other. When one of them starts stumbling in the boat and getting tangles on every other cast... the alcohol consumption needs to be questioned. For these guys, I think that a red-and-white bobber, not nymphing, would have been a better fit for them. Luckily, these types of guys are very few and far between in the fly-fishing world, and most anglers can handle a good drink.

See, alcohol and fly fishing are made for each other. A perfect match made on the river. Drinking and fly fishing are not a necessity, but then again neither is that cup of coffee we all enjoy in the morning. Coffee, just like alcohol in fly fishing, makes the day go better. A cold beer, a warm swig of whiskey, or even a blended margarita can turn your river refuge into paradise. So, the next time you go fly fishing, grab some beers and a few friends and go create some memories. Just make sure you're in a state of mind that allows you to remember them.

SOUTHERN COMFORT

It's never a good start to my day when I pull up to the boat launch and find my clients are still intoxicated from the night before.

Leaving the bar at 2 o'clock in the morning is a terrible decision when you have a 6 o'clock meet time with your guide. Stumbling on solid ground doesn't bode well for standing in a moving boat. Guiding hung-over people is one of the worst experiences for a fishing guide because no one wants to be there. The client is hurting and regretting his decision to do multiple rounds of God-knows-what shots with his buddies the night before, while the guide knows that no amount of his expertise and skill will have any bearing on the way the day unfolds. The trip becomes a crapshoot before it even begins. Emphasis on "crap." I have numerous stories about guiding hung-over clients, but there's one that trumps them all.

My good friend and I were guiding four clients on the Sacramento River one day in June. The weather was warm, the sky was blue, and the water was cold. When we pulled up to the boat launch, we were met by three middle-aged men, all clients Cindy had brought out. She was an insurance broker in her late 30s. As we approached, I noticed how giddy they all were—laughing, making sarcastic remarks to each other, just having a great time. I thought it was odd for them to have that much energy so early in the morning—until I noticed that one of them was holding a big bottle of Southern Comfort.

It turns out they had left the bar just three hours earlier and were still feeling the effects of a full night of drinking. Before these folks got into our trucks to drive to the starting point, they wanted to do a celebratory shot to start the day. So, one by one, they each took a solid pull off the bottle, and then had one big group hug. Now they were ready for the day. I was guiding Bob and Cindy. Of course, Bob was the last to take a shot of SoCo, and he ended up with the bottle.

As we drove, Bob, Cindy, and I had a good conversation about life and the river...and all the while Bob continued to take swigs from the bottle. This continued once we got to the river, and I prepped the boat and rods for the day.

Once I got the boat in the water, I gave Cindy a quick fly-fishing lesson, as this was her first time. I pulled the boat over into a riffle and began to teach her the basics of fly casting, mending, and setting the hook. I should note that between her looks and her personality, many men would be attracted to Cindy—including, evidently, Bob. As Cindy learned how to cast, Bob gave her flirtatious encouragement while he continued to drink from the whiskey bottle like a toddler with a sippy cup. Cindy smiled and thanked him, but I could tell she knew as well as I did that Bob was getting hammered.

Cindy finally got up to speed and was ready to start fly fishing. I pulled up the anchor and rowed down to our first fishing spot. I told Cindy and Bob to get ready to cast off the right side of the boat into a shallow riffle. They both pulled their flies off and started to cast. Cindy made a great cast right to the perfect spot in the run. Bob, on the other hand, whipped his line into a miserable tangle. I told Bob to take a seat and then fished Cindy through the run.

Right in the bucket Cindy got a hard strike and quickly set the hook on a beautiful and feisty rainbow trout. She remembered all that I had taught her, keeping her rod high, stripping her line, letting the fish run, and then slowly lifting the trout toward the net. After we released the fish, Cindy gave me a big smile and a high five.

Then I untangled Bob's line and rowed back to the top of the riffle to see if we could catch another fish. Cindy made another great cast. Bob, once again, sloppily whipped his rod back and forth, resulting in another massive tangle. Cindy fished her drift out and was rewarded with her second rainbow trout of the day.

I rowed over to the edge of the riffle and began working on Bob's bird nest. I warned them it was going to take a while. So Bob began to chat up Cindy. They were having a friendly conversation at first, but then the liquid courage started to take hold of Bob's mental state.

"Cindy, you are a beautiful woman," he said out of the blue.

Cindy looked back at Bob and warmly smiled at him.

"Thank you," she replied.

"Cindy, you are really beautiful!" Bob continued. "I bet your mom must be attractive too. A beautiful woman like you doesn't come from ugly parents. I bet your mother is close to my age. How old is your mom, Cindy?"

Cindy, now annoyed with Bob's drunkenness and looking to end the conversation, said, "She is good-looking. She's 59 and single. I love my mom deeply. We have a great relationship. She's one of my best friends."

Bob nodded his head as he listened to Cindy's response.

"Is there any chance you'd be willing to introduce your mother and me? It would be fun to go on a blind date with her," Bob said.

Cindy shook her head no and laughed softly. "I don't think that's going to happen."

"Why not, Cindy? I'm a good guy. I have a great job, I'm fairly attractive, I'm single, I'll show her a great time. You know, some women would consider me a great catch," Bob said.

"Sorry, Bob. Not gonna happen," Cindy replied. "I don't think the two of you would be good together."

"Cindy, give me a chance here," Bob said aggressively.

"I don't understand your fascination with my mother," said Cindy, now even more annoyed. "You've never even met her before."

"Well, Cindy, it's pretty simple," said Bob. "I really just want to f**k your mom!"

I'd heard enough. "Wow, man. That is not okay to say," I told him. "I think you're done drinking for the day. You've had a week's worth of whiskey in the last two hours."

I reached for the bottle, but Bob beat me to it.

"Gimme the bottle, Bob. Time for you to stop," I told him.

"You are way past your limit. If you want me to guide you any more today, you will hand me that Southern Comfort."

Bob quickly took another shot from the bottle and then begrudgingly handed it to me.

After this awkward moment, the boat got uncomfortably quiet. No one spoke and the only sound was the lapping waves in the river. I continued to work on Bob's tangle, and after a few more minutes we were ready to go again.

The two of them stood up to get ready for the third cast of the day. Cindy, trying to focus on the fishing rather than Bob's stupid statement, made another great cast. Bob, too, was finally able to get a decent cast off. We went through the riffle our third time with no luck, and headed to the next spot about five minutes downriver.

As I rowed, Bob announced he was getting tired and was going to take a little rest. He slowly lowered himself to the floor of the drift boat and contorted his body to somehow fit in the awkward space between his seat and the leg braces. Within a minute Bob was asleep, lying twisted in the back of the boat; his arm, still holding onto his rod, hung over the side.

My better judgement told me I should grab his rod and reel it up for him so he wouldn't lose his thousand dollar combo. On the other hand, this could be a great learning experience for Bob. If his rod got snagged on a log and ripped out of his hand, maybe he would think twice about his alcohol consumption. So, I decided to leave it. There went his line, dragging 40 feet behind us.

Just before we got to the next spot, Bob's line went tight. To my dismay, it wasn't a snag but rather a fish. Somehow, his dangling fly line trolling behind the boat enticed the dumbest fish in the river. Bob instantly woke up and lifted his arm.

"Fish on!" he yelled.

As he struggled to stand up, he began to fall out of the boat. I quickly jumped up and grabbed him before he tumbled into the water. No longer able to stand by himself, Bob was somehow able to hold onto his rod and keep the fish on. After several minutes, Bob reeled in a nice two-pound trout.

Ecstatic about his catch, Bob gave me a big high five. "That was awesome!"

And…after taking in his moment of glory, he turned his attention back to Cindy.

"Cindy, you're lookin' great up there," he said. "You are a beautiful woman. Man, everything about you is just perfect. Your blonde hair…tan skin…cute outfit… Any guy would be lucky to go out with you. Any chance I could take you out one night?"

Cindy glared at him. "That is *not* happening," she said. "There is *zero* chance I will ever go on a date with you."

"Come on, Cindy," Bob persisted, with that liquid courage still flowing through his veins. "We could make a great couple."

"Nope. Never happening!" Cindy replied.

"Well, if you won't go on a date with me, could we just hook up?" Bob asked.

I'd heard enough.

"You have to stop this, man," I told him. "First you try to get with her mom. Now you're trying to get with her. Not okay. What you're doing is very disrespectful. For your own dignity, you need to stop talking."

"Ryan, we're all friends here," Bob replied. "We're all okay.

I'm sorry, Cindy. I shouldn't have said those things. I think I've had too much to drink. The whiskey has taken away my good judgement."

Finally, it seemed Bob had come to his senses.

"Well," he continued, "if you won't go out with me, can you at least show me your boobies?"

Or not.

Cindy didn't respond. She just stared down the river in complete silence.

"I'm sorry this is happening to you," I told Cindy. "This is really bad. I think we should catch up to your other friends and get you out of this boat. This has to end."

Cindy nodded in agreement. I quickly started to row down the river to catch up to the other boat. After a very long 10 minutes, I pulled alongside and told them that Bob needed to go home. They all looked at him swaying back and forth in his chair and agreed. Cindy got into the other boat and we began the long, nine-mile row to the takeout.

Bob had managed to ruin the day for his friends. In addition to enduring relentless harassment, poor Cindy's first fly-fishing experience lasted all of three casts—fortunately, she caught fish on two of them.

For my buddy and me, we got a short day on the river and got back to our families earlier than expected. Plus, I got another amazing story to tell, though I hope you see Bob as a cautionary tale. Next time you go fishing, try not to show up drunk. If you do, at least leave the Southern Comfort in the car.

THE ONE FLY TOURNAMENT

Tensions in the valley have been rising for weeks.

One of the world's largest fly-fishing tournaments, The One Fly Tournament, is just around the corner. I'm preparing to experience it for the first time.

Every fall, anglers from around the world descend on little Jackson Hole, Wyoming to try their luck in this two-day tournament. Teams of four from Italy, New Zealand, Australia, and across the United States come to compete and raise money for charity. The challenge that lies before every guide and angler is this: each angler only gets one fly per day. If you lose your fly in a bush, if it gets hung up on a rock, if you break it off in a trout's mouth, if the fly unravels, if the hook breaks, or if a bat eats it in midair, you are *out* of the tourney for that day. With a $6,000 entry fee, plus travel expenses, the last thing a competing angler can afford to do is lose his or her one precious little fly.

The big question is, if you only have one fly to fish for an entire day, which one do you pick?

For weeks, guides have secretly been tying their favorite patterns, sitting at their benches in the dark with only a fly-tying light and a bottle of bourbon to keep them company. This is where guides start having visions of big, white mouths slurping down their favorite flies.

From fly tying desks all over the world, secret weapons emerge on that first morning of the tournament. The creations come out as bombproof masterpieces, with double coats of head cement to ensure no thread can come loose. Strong hooks are a must. Extra pieces of foam and deer hair are added to make sure that each dry fly will ride high to the very end. Every piece of material, hook, and thread is scrutinized. This fly has to be perfect.

But in the end, it's all up to the anglers. A guide can spend days creating the perfect fly, only to have an angler decide to fish his own creation. They might even decide to fish a red San Juan worm! That might sound hilarious, but someone actually won the One Fly Tournament with that exact fly several years ago. For Day One of this year's tournament, I'm planning to suggest a size-16 PMD Challenged Emerger. The PMD hatch during the middle of the day has been huge, and the Challenged Emerger is the one fly I have the most confidence in. For weeks, I've thought about this fly selection, and as I drive up to the competitors' hotel, I have all my fingers and toes crossed, hoping my fishermen go with my suggestion.

I pull up to the hotel lobby and take a quiet moment in my truck. The whole valley is buzzing this morning. Drift boats are everywhere, guides are having secret meetings about where to fish, and of course, those flies are hidden out of sight. As I sit in my truck, I tell myself, "This is just another guide day. Go about this day like you would any other."

In order to qualify for the Head Guide Award, I need my anglers to catch and measure six 16-inch trout each…and, of course, keep their flies. If they can do that, we will easily be in the top three spots. The personal pep talk sounds great in my head, but then I remember it all depends on who I have in my boat. All guides dream of being assigned a master angler who can cast the fly anywhere it needs to go and get the perfect drift into a willing trout's mouth. I take a depth breath, but as I exhale, I still have some nerves.

I walk into the lobby of the hotel. There, sitting on a cold, hard, pine-tree-log bench, is a woman and a man, both in their 60's, waiting for their guide. No friendly conversation this morning —each is focused on the task at hand. They have their rod tubes across their laps and their gear bags set on the ground at hand, ready to go.

I walk over to them and introduce myself. The man is Bill, from the Australian team. This team of 4 anglers flies over from Sydney every year to compete against some of the best fly fishers in the world. This is Bill's seventh One Fly Tournament, and as I look at his aged, sun-kissed face and misty blue eyes, I can tell he thinks this will be the year his team takes the trophy home.

The woman is Gail, from the Nebraska team. She has pale skin, large glasses, and a wide-brimmed straw hat with a red bow. Gail is a veteran of this tournament; she and three girl-friends have been competing together for 12 years straight. Fortunately, I have a pair of anglers who are familiar with the event, though I'm crossing my toes that they know how to fish.

You're probably wondering why anglers from two different teams fish together. Well, if there's a common trait among fishermen, it's that we're all liars. Whether it's about the size of the fish or how many we caught, we all tend to stretch the truth. So, the One Fly Committee decided it best to have members from different teams fish with each other to keep everyone honest.

After we introduce ourselves, I'm eager to know if Bill and Gail have chosen to fish their own flies or if they'll be going with my suggestion.

"I plan on fishing a small, size-12 stonefly dry called the J-Slam," says Bill with a smile.

"How do you know about that fly?" I ask, surprised by his answer.

Bill tells me he's been pre-fishing the tournament with the head guide of my lodge the past four days. Inside I'm jumping up and down, yelling, "Hooray! Hooray! I didn't get a chump for an angler!" The J-Slam is the ultimate secret weapon—a small, tan stonefly with a mix of foam, bear hair, and small rubber legs. And somehow, I've been granted access to it. I tell Bill that I'm familiar with this fly, and I am one-hundred-percent supportive of his selection. Actually, I'm stoked.

Then I look over to Gail. She shares that she, too, has been pre-fishing and chose her secret…streamer. Instantly, I'm scratching my head and thinking about the weather. Gail digs into her pocket to show me the fly. No doubt, the trout on the South Fork of the Snake love to eat streamers, but streamers are usually best under dark conditions—early in the morning, under heavy cloud cover, or during rain. Today's forecast is for blue skies and 85 degrees.

She finally gets the fly unhooked from all the strings in her pocket. My first impression is that it should be called the "USC Trojan Fly" due to the red, gold, and white flashabou tied around the hook. There are no other materials besides thread holding it all together. I hold it in my hand, and I have to admit, I'm impressed by the simple, creative thought put into it. No doubt, the huge flash effect will get the attention of every trout in the river—but will it attract them or scare them all away?

I suggest to Gail that she *not* use the streamer due to the warm, clear weather we're expecting. She looks down at the fly in her hand.

"I have a lot of faith in this fly," she says. "It's produced some really nice fish the last two days on the river."

I think back on the last two days' weather and recall it was the same as it is now.

"You did well streamer fishing the last two days?" I ask her. "If you don't mind me asking, how would you define 'well'?" I just have to check.

"I caught two trout yesterday, and three the day before that," Gail says.

I can't hold back my smirk.

"Gail, two or three fish is not winning this tournament," I say. "We need to use a fly that will catch more fish than that."

"The ones I caught were all really big," she tells me.

If she caught a couple of monster brown trout, that would make up for not reaching the goal of six 16-inch trout.

"Okay. How big were those trout?" I ask.

"I landed one 19-inch brown and one 18-inch cutthroat," Gail says.

"Those are great fish, but they are not big for this river," I say. "My plan was to fish a PMD Challenged Emerger. You can catch the same sized fish on this fly, plus you'll have 10 times the opportunities as you would with that streamer."

Gail looks up at me with defeat in her eyes. I'm pretty sure this was the moment she lost faith in me as a guide. She looks back at her flashy streamer.

"Okay," she says, "let me see the fly you're suggesting."

I hand her the size-16 PMD Emerger with an elk hair post, a small piece of pink dubbing, and a pheasant tail body. This fly is deadly as it hangs in the film. It's like the bug is trying to hatch. Gail takes one look at it and starts shaking her head no.

"I won't be able to see that fly," she tells me. "My eyes are old. I need something bigger."

"As long as I can see the fly, that's all that matters," I tell her. "I know it will be hard for you, but this fly has caught 95 percent of my fish the last three weeks. Right now, in these conditions, it's an absolute killer pattern."

"Well, I had a backup plan in case you didn't think the streamer was a good idea."

Gail bends down and starts digging through her collection of fly boxes in her gear bag. After a few minutes of opening and closing box after box, she stands up with a size-8 Parachute Adams in her hand. This fly, which is supposed to represent many different forms of smaller mayflies, is bigger than Bill's stonefly imitation.

It is the Godzilla of Parachute Adams.

In over twenty years of fly fishing, I have never seen a Parachute Adams tied this big. Her eyes must be *really* bad. Even a dumb brook trout in a high-mountain lake that sees only a handful of flies each summer wouldn't eat this thing. Maybe we should do a thread check on this fly–see if it's been using performance-enhancing drugs.

I politely keep all these comments to myself.

"I think a Parachute Adams would be a great choice," I tell her. "It just needs to be something smaller, like a 14 or 16."

I know this fly will not do as well as the PMD I'm suggesting. But it will do a good enough job to keep her in the running.

"Okay, let me see what else I have in here," Gail says dejectedly.

At this point in the fly selection process, I can tell Gail is at a loss. Her young rookie One Fly guide has now shot down two of her ideas. After a few more minutes she pops up again.

"What about this one?" she asks.

This time Gail is holding a size-8 Elk Hair Caddis. I look down at the fly and then back up at her hopeful face while shaking my head no.

"We have the same problem here," I say. "This fly selection is not bad, but the pattern itself is too large. Trout on the South Fork of the Snake see a lot of flies every summer, and we need something more realistic. How about an Elk Hair Caddis in a 16 or 18? I know we would do really well with that fly."

There aren't many four-inch caddis flying around, that I'm aware of. If there's somewhere in the world having consistent hatches of four-inch caddis, I want to fish *that* river. Please send me the coordinates.

"I can't see flies that small…I'm worried I won't do well," she reminds me.

"Every week I have someone who can't see or find their fly, and we always tend to do well," I assure her. "As long as you can listen and set the hook when I tell you to, we'll do just fine."

Gail asks to see my PMD pattern a second time. After inspecting the fly for a couple minutes, and looking for other monstrous things to use, she begrudgingly agrees to go with my suggestion.

Now I'm really excited. I have all the confidence in the world as I gather up their gear and start heading to the truck. As we get in, Bill's and my excitement is palpable, but Gail seems lost in her thoughts. Maybe I should have just let her go with her beloved Trojan streamer. As I start driving, I look in the rearview mirror and see a woman who has replaced her passion with doubt.

When we get to the river, I start putting the rods and boat together and tell Bill and Gail my game plan.

"We have two different types of flies to fish today," I say. "Bill, your fly will work best in the morning when the light is low. Gail, your PMD will start working about 11 o'clock when the hatch starts. So, to start off the day, Bill, you fish the front of the boat. Gail, you're in the back. Now, Gail, I need you to be patient for the first couple of hours; your fly won't see any action. However, in the middle to later parts of the day, you're gonna have the perfect fly, so you'll move to the front. Does that sound good and fair to you guys?"

Both agree it's a strong plan. I finish rigging rods and get the boat in the water.

I pull out my phone to check the time. We can't start fishing until 8 o'clock. 10 minutes to go. I am fired up. I haven't felt this much excitement and energy since my first bonefishing trip in Mexico.

After what seems like enough time to complete a marathon, our adventure begins.

The first bank of the day is a good one. It's a very fishy spot with lots of morning shade and large boulders for fish to hide behind. This is literally the perfect spot for Bill to fish that small stonefly. "Get ready," I tell them both. They start pulling line off their reels and prepare for their first casts.

"As soon as we come around the next bush, we want to cast those flies right on the seam line between the slack water and the current," I say.

Bill starts his cast.

To my absolute horror, he sticks his fly in the bush. It breaks off.

"Really, Bill!? The first cast!? That was one expensive fly!" I yell.

Just kidding. That didn't happen. However, I do know two guides who had anglers lose their flies within the first five minutes of the tournament. Talk about brutal.

We aren't ten minutes into our morning before Bill has a nice rainbow blow up on his fly. He sets the hook, and the fight is on. A couple minutes later, a beautiful 17-inch rainbow hits the net. We decide to measure the fish, and just like that, we're on the scoreboard.

Five minutes later, he has a 16-inch cutthroat on the line. Bill once again plays the fish correctly, and we score our second trout of the morning. About 10 minutes after that, Bill follows up with an 18-inch cutthroat. Then he misses three smaller fish before he puts everything together again.

The next fish rises slowly from the grassy bank. It sticks its nose out to let that fly float into the death trap. Another good hookset and fight puts the second 18-inch cutty on the scorecard. By this point I feel like things can't get any better.

My stonefly rod is pounding them, and Gail has one of the best afternoon flies out there. Oh, man, please let this strong momentum continue.

We go to a bank I don't fish very often, but I know it has some big browns in it. I decide to give up on numbers of fish and try to find a big one. Bill starts checking every nook and cranny on the bank when, suddenly, he gets the "toilet flush." The toilet flush is when your fly suddenly disappears and all you see is a splash on the water the size of a bowling ball. It's a big trout creating such a strong suction of water that the fish eats your fly without showing any part of its body. All you see is a huge bubble exploding on the surface of the water and the fly suddenly disappears!

After the toilet flush, Bill fires back with a firm hookset. The rod surges back and forth from strong, purposeful head shakes. Quickly, the fish runs out to the middle of the river, and the chase is ON. I run down the fish with my boat. Within three or four minutes, a beautiful *22-inch* brown hits the net.

Now I'm freaking out: It's about 10 o'clock. I have one angler with five of his six fish landed. And most of them are bigger than my original goal.

But I can tell Gail is starting to get frustrated as she watches Bill have a successful morning.

"Hang in there," I tell her. "It's not your time yet. In about an hour you're really gonna start doing some damage."

She nods her head and gets back to casting. Over the next hour, Bill lands several more fish, but they're all in the 15- to 16-inch class. I want to make sure we save our last spot for a good-sized trout. Bill agrees and goes on the hunt for another big brown to finish off his day.

Right around 11 o'clock, I have Gail and Bill switch spots. Bill is still catching quite a few fish, but I start to see the first signs of a PMD hatch. Small, light-pink PMDs start fluttering through the air and gliding across the surface of the water. As the hatch starts, I know I need to be a little farther downriver to hit all the good, foamy PMD water. A couple miles down, we get to a long, slow flat with some nice fish sitting up in the shallow, glassy part of the run. These fish are in about a foot of water, waiting for small mayflies to float down to their snouts. As I look downriver, I can see several small rings popping under the surface of the water.

"We have a handful of trout eating emergers about 100 feet downriver," I warn Gail.

She turns her attention to the rising fish, and as we approach them, she makes an effortless 40-foot cast that slowly falls to the water. Her fly floats about 15 feet before a small nose pops up and sucks in her fly. Gail gently sets the hook, trying not to break the tippet, and as the fish feels the hook point drive into its hard, fleshy mouth, it surges out of the water.

"Easy, Gail, that's a good one! Take your time," I tell her. "That looks like about a 24-inch brown just ate your fly. Let that fish run! Don't horse it."

The brown trout zips out to the middle of the river. Like with Bill's big brown, we go to chase it down. Within a couple minutes, the fish has started to calm. Now it's just swimming around the boat. Gail does an excellent job. I can tell she's a veteran when it comes to playing and landing fish. Near the end of the battle, the brown trout starts to give up.

"Okay, Gail, let's try lifting that fish up," I say. "But make sure you don't hold too tightly to the line in case the fish wants to take off again."

"Yep, I've done this a few times," she responds.

The fish starts heading our way. Gail strips in her last couple feet of line and then starts lifting the fish toward the net. About two feet from the net, the brown gives one last kick toward the bottom.

"Let it go! Let it go!" I yell. "Give it line, Gail!"

But it's too late.

The rod flings back from the recoil of breaking the line. There is absolute silence. Gail slowly lowers into her chair, her rod drooping from her limp hands, as her head drops to her leg brace. Bill and I glance at each other; we know we'd better not say anything. Gail made the same mistake we've all made—trying to get the fish to the net before the fish is ready. If she had let it run one more time, we probably would have landed it the next time it came to the boat. One more minute and she would've had a great fish to start the day.

And she would still have her fly.

As we quietly float down the river, Gail gazes out over the water. I imagine she's replaying each moment of the fight in her head. To add insult to injury, as we go around the next corner, there are 10 to 12 big, healthy rainbows and cutthroats rising to PMD emergers in the first foam hole of the day. Gail would have hammered the fish in this hole if she still had her fly.

Bill tries his luck, but these trout are so dialed in to those small mayflies that the stonefly actually puts them down. Within a matter of minutes, I go from hoping for the Top Guide Award to having an angler with a Day One score of big fat zero. Bill could still post a great score, but I was finished. It didn't matter if I had a good score with Bill and an epic second day—Gail's small mistake came with giant consequences.

Now Bill and I think it's time to give her some encouragement. "You can fish, Gail," I tell her, though nothing will count for the tournament now. Gail decides to tie on her special streamer to see how she would have done with her first option. Bill hops back into the front of the boat, and we go searching for one more big fish to complete his scorecard. We focus on faster, rocky banks as we look for aggressive rises and willing fish. Bill lands a few more, but none good enough to fill the last spot. So I tell him we'll go fish the cliff walls; there are always big fish underneath them.

As we approach the first wall, Bill casts his fly within inches of the rock. A 20-inch cutthroat rises to look at his fly but refuses to take it. Bill throws a second good cast up there and gets another refusal. Then a third. Then a fourth. By this point my arms and back are starting to get tired from holding the boat in place.

"Bill, hold that next cast," I say. "It's obvious there's something about your fly that fish doesn't like. We'll go around the corner to the next set of cliffs."

As I stop rowing to give my arms a rest, Bill decides to throw one last desperate cast toward the wall...and his fly finds a small bush about 15 feet above the water.

"Oh, noooo!" I moan. *Shit.*

I quickly stroke as hard as I can on the oars. *Stroke. Stroke. Stroke.* Watching the cliff, I can see my boat's not moving. I'm not gaining any ground.

"Rip off your line to give it slack," I yell at him. "I have to go all the way across the river to get into that soft current and see if I can make it back up."

By the time I get to the other side of the river, Bill's got about 100 feet of backing hanging off his rod tip. I start to row back up the eddy…and here comes another drift boat, heading directly for Bill's line. *Shit.*

"WATCH THE LINE!" I yell desperately. "Please try not to break it off! We're in the One Fly!"

We're watching the boat inch toward Bill's line. I'm thinking there's no way this boat doesn't break Bill's line. Both of us are shaking our heads in disbelief as, one by one, they gingerly grab the line, passing it overhead from one angler to the next across the boat, being careful to not break it. Finally, they've passed through, and the line…drops back into the water.

"WOW, that was lucky," I tell Bill. But there's no time to celebrate. We've gotta get that fly.

I start rowing across the river, putting my whole strength into each pull on the oars. *Stroke. Stroke. Stroke.* It's getting hard. My muscles are burning; I'm losing some ground. By the time I get back to the cliff, I'm in the exact same spot and too far downriver to gain any ground. *Shit.*

After about two minutes of grunting and grimacing, I tell Bill, breathless, "You better hope that leader's gonna hold. I can't do any more here. Pull hard on that rod." *Stroke. Stroke. Stroke.* Bill hesitates.

"Pull! Pull! Come on, buddy, I'm running outta gas here!"

Reluctantly, Bill pulls hard on the line. It comes out of the bush and falls to the water. To my dismay, the fly is gone—still stuck in the bush 15 feet above the water, glistening in the sun. There was nothing more I could have done.

The "just one more cast" mindset has bit Bill straight in the ass. He's bummed out that his almost-perfect day has disappeared with the loss of his fly. He isn't heartbroken like Gail because he's still got the epic morning on his scorecard. I'm feeling frustration and peace at the same time. All of a sudden, this has turned into just a normal guide day—just like I told myself in the truck hours earlier.

Bill decides to tie on a new J-Slam, the same type of fly he'd lost, and fish it until the end of the day. He manages to land another 20-inch brown near the end of our drift. Gail, on the other hand, fishes her flashy streamer the rest of the day and never once gets a follow. I'm not sure what would've been better for Gail—to pick a fly that didn't catch a fish or to settle on a smaller fly she lost early in the day. I guess only Gail knows.

Most guides say the One Fly Tournament is all about the anglers you get in your boat. I never completely understood that theory. Until that day. I had some really good anglers, and like most of us, they made some mistakes. Sometimes we rush to land a fish, or we try one more cast into a dangerous spot. But isn't that the fun part of the sport? If we all went out on the water and did everything perfectly every time, took no risks, we wouldn't be challenged.

What if Gail landed that huge brown trout? What if Bill's last cast actually caught that beautiful cutthroat? I would be writing a different kind of story, that's for sure. The beauty of fly fishing is we never know whether "one more cast" will catch a big fish or the bush hanging above it. Hopefully, next time, it'll be the fish.

ONE FLY LEGENDS

You know what five summers of guiding on the South Fork of the Snake will get you? I've heard tales so great, they have become legend in this small, tight-knit fly fishing community. Some of these stories make me wonder: Are they complete myths? Partial truths? True stories of magical guides in direct contact with the fly-fishing gods? Every summer, when the world-famous One Fly Tournament comes to the valley, whispers of these stories touch clients' ears and make their jaws drop.

Keep in mind, each contestant in this two-day, four-person team, fly fishing tournament is allowed just one fly per day. If you lose your fly or break the hook, you are out for that day. The last thing you want to do when you fly across the world to participate in the One Fly is cast that precious fly into a tree or snap it off on your back cast.

Many years ago, a guide convinced his two competitors to use small PMD emergers as their weapons of choice. They had a slow morning, as expected with a midday hatch, but by lunchtime they were staged up in a famous riffle. It's no secret spot, known by many regulars on the river. As the PMD hatch starts, the riffle comes alive with groups of glistening noses. The first to rise are the cutthroat trout. Then, dark-green rainbow submarines arise from the dark-colored water to partake in the feast. There, before the two anglers' eyes, sit more than 20 happily feeding cutthroats and rainbows.

This sight alone would send even the most veteran anglers into an excited fury, but it's the One Fly. Every single cast carries tremendous weight and meaning. One wrong move, and you're out. So the competitors decide to take turns casting to fish. They catch a couple. Then, the worst that could happen? It happens.

One angler casts to a 20-inch cutthroat and makes the mistake of setting the hook too hard. Instantly, the tippet breaks and the cutthroat, in an agitated mood, violently shakes his head and disappears into the depths. Every cuss word in the book comes out, and his frustration brings him to his knees on the rough, dirty floor of the boat. The realization of losing his fly and being out of the tournament for the rest of the day torments him. He has let himself and his team down. The chance of being Top Angler (and his team winning the tournament) has been left behind in the mouth of a willing cutty at the bottom of the river. If only he had one more chance to try it over again.

The guide gently puts his hand on the angler's shoulder. "My friend, do not fret," says the guide. "There is still hope."

The angler turns to him with a confused and glazed look. "What do you mean?" he asks.

"The fish you hooked was a really nice cutthroat," says the guide. "That fish has been in this riffle for months. I've hooked him more than 20 times. I'm about ready to give that fish a name. I haven't decided yet, but I was thinking maybe 'Freddy.'"

"Okay, that's great and all, but how does that get my fly back?" asks the angler.

"Well, that fish has to eat at some point," says the guide. "Right now, the PMD hatch is the biggest food source, and it won't be long before that fish has the guts to come back up and start rising again."

So, the three of them sit there for 45 minutes, staring into the riffle– not fishing or casting. Then, sure enough, Freddy the Cutthroat decides to move back into the slot to start feeding again. The guide quickly points out the trout and instructs the other angler to start fishing for Freddy. On his fourth cast, he hooks him. But this time is different; Freddy is hooked and landed with precision. And there, in the top part of his lip, is the PMD emerger that had been broken off just an hour before!

Freddy had done everyone a solid favor. He returned the lost fly to the first angler, and the second angler added a beautiful fish to his scorecard. In an unexpected turn of events, both anglers were fishing in the tournament again. Yes, the fly was lost, but the rules state that if the original fly is recovered, the angler can start fishing again.

All these years later, Freddy still lives in that riffle. Age has made him even bigger and wiser. Everyone knows how he once came to the aid of a desperate fly fisherman.

The second story is one of Persistence. The ability to fish

hard throughout the day can sometimes really pay off. This particular year, the tournament had some strong competition. After the first day, there were a handful of teams neck-and-neck, trying to claw their way to the top. One measured fish was the only thing between first and fourth place. Each fish landed on the second day would bring a team one step closer to fame.

The fishing on the first day of the tournament was awesome, with lots of fish caught and measured—the biggest being 21 inches. One of the guides in the tournament was famous for nymphing, and for many years had convinced all his anglers that a nymph was the way to go. Many people still disagree with him, but with a previous victory as Top Guide in the One Fly, it's hard not to acknowledge how deadly nymphing can be. This particular guide sat in third place after the first day of the tournament. However, the fishing on the second day was much more challenging than the first.

On the second day, the fish were there and feeding, but they were not dialed into one pattern. Like many of the other guides, the nymph expert was exasperated. He kept believing in his system, though, and was fishing every nook and cranny he knew, trying to find a few willing fish. As the second day was winding down, the guide decided to fish one more bank. With 15 minutes to go, he had one of the best rock-and-foam banks left on the river and instructed both of his clients to cast their orange indicators up against the rocky bank. He knew this was a risky move, as they both could potentially lose their flies, but he decided it was a "no guts, no glory" moment.

The anglers mended their lines and started fishing the bank. The first stretch of the bank produced nothing. As they approached the last hundred yards in the drift, a monstrous

24-inch rainbow rocketed out of the water, trying to eat the indicator. The fish swam so fast and hard at the indicator that it threw its enormous body out of the water, completely missing its target—and landing in their boat, 10 feet away. There, in the bottom of the boat, was a thrashing, frustrated, and confused six-pound rainbow!

That fish shocked everyone in the boat. The angler in the front bent over and put the hook in the fish's mouth.

"That's in the boat, Bob. Game over," says the angler. "Thank you, fish. I believe you just won me the One Fly."

The guide quickly takes the hand-placed hook out of the fish's mouth, measures the fish, and releases it back to the water. Within seconds the laughter starts rolling, the cigars come out, and the tournament ends. This rocket fish was not only the largest fish "landed" in the tournament, it also secured another win for the nympho-maniac guide.

Guess it shows you that you truly never know what might happen on any given day. On this day, the fish gods air-mailed a One Fly victory in the form of one robust rainbow.

The last legend shows the incredible distance a guide will go to continue to compete in the One Fly. Everybody knows the importance of a good, durable fly in this tournament. Everything from the materials to the tie and hook are extremely important. Heavy-wire hooks and big, bushy flies are the norm. This legendary guide was ready for anything and everything, literally following the Boy Scout motto of "Be Prepared."

But today, everything was going wrong with the guide's fly. He had decided to use a large, foam Chernobyl Ant pattern—a great choice in terms of longevity and larger hook size. Things were going great until he noticed some thread dangling off the head of the fly. Near the eye of the hook, the thread was starting to unravel. After a quick look at the fly and tying a small half hitch with the thread, he digs into his gear bag and pulls out a bottle of super glue. He puts a small drop of glue on the loose thread and then lets it set for 15 minutes. After it hardens, it looks like the fly is ready to go again.

The fly fishes well for another hour, but after it gets eaten several times, the thread in the middle of the body comes unraveled. By the time he catches the faltering fly, the foam-bodied stonefly is barely holding on, with just a couple wraps of thread.

The guide quickly pulls the boat over to the side of the river and drops his anchor. He stands up and starts digging through his storage compartment under his seat. After a few moments, the guide pulls out a vise, stand, bobbin, and other tools.

The One Fly rules state that you can't add any new materials to the fly, but fixing a fly with its original materials is allowed. This guide quickly takes the fly apart and carefully unravels each wrap of thread as he winds it back onto a spare empty thread spool. Then, using the original thread, he reties a modified version of the Chernobyl Ant.

He gets the fly sturdy enough to last for a few more hours—he thinks–just enough time to compete to the end. With only three hours left in the contest, whatever life they get out of this fly is a bonus. About half an hour later, the angler sets the hook too hard. The hook point breaks off in the mouth of a fish. But the team doesn't notice the broken hook right away. A couple missed fish and they figure out something's not right. The guide takes a look at the hook and knows they're finished.

But wait! He has an idea. After contemplating the situation for a couple minutes, he gets on his phone and calls one of his best friends. "Meet me at the nearest access point. And bring an electric grinder," he says. Thirty minutes later, his friend shows up with a generator, an extension cord, and the grinder. The sacred fly goes into the vise, and they carefully grind a new hook point.

The angler gets back to it. He continues to use the battered and worn fly until the end of the day. Many fish are lost due to the funky new hook, but he does land a few.

In the end, his team didn't win the tournament. But the guide's ingenuity turned him into a legend. He raised the bar for every guide and angler to come. This story will no doubt outlive the guide; one day, my daughter will tell this legend as she floats down the mighty South Fork of the Snake.

There is something truly magical about the One Fly. Legends are created. Techniques are tested. Strategy is thrown out the window. All the stars must align if you want to emerge victorious. People flood the Swan Valley for this event every year with good reason. Every day on the water presents another chance at a story that will inspire anglers for generations to come.

ALL NATURAL

Memorable moments are experienced all the time on the river. An angler might have several over the course of a day. Maybe it's a big fish brought to hand…or even one that breaks off. It could be watching a loved one catch his or her first fish on a fly. Falling in the river certainly counts as a memorable moment. So does getting stuck in a massive thunderstorm and being hailed on for three hours straight (believe me, that totally sucks).

For guides, truly memorable moments don't stand out as readily as they do for our clients. Yes, we remember the funny stories, or the occasional monstrous fish, but the day in, day out nature of our work tends to cause individual moments to bleed together in our life's painting.

One summer day in Idaho, though, I had a client I will never forget. I keep trying to shake the image of him from my head, but I'm convinced this particular angler will haunt my memory forever.

It started off like any normal guide day. I pull up to the fly shop at the lodge, walk in, and greet my client: a tall, slender guy in his mid-40's. Let's call him Ziggy. (I realize that's an odd alias, but believe me, it totally fits.) Ziggy wears a pair of wire-rimmed glasses and has a neatly trimmed but full beard with splashes of gray. Wiry brown curls tweak haphazardly out of his head. He's wearing light green cargo pants, a polo shirt, a brown tweed jacket, and a light cashmere scarf around his neck. I reflexively do a double-take. Ziggy is not dressed like the typical fly fisherman I encounter at this lodge. Instead, he looks like a well-to-do, clean-cut hippy. I'm thinking a professor of botany at a liberal arts college.

Heading to the river in my truck, Ziggy and I have a pleasant conversation about fishing, the ecology of the river, and the special things we'll see that day. This was Ziggy's first time in Idaho, and he wanted to learn as much as possible about the area. So I decided to float the upper stretches of the South Fork of the Snake River to give Ziggy the full experience. I'm hoping we get some good fishing and see some exciting wildlife, and I'm looking forward to showing him the famous Falls Creek Falls waterfall.

It's not long before my first impression of Ziggy is confirmed. He's an educated man—a pharmacist by trade—and he loves being immersed in nature. He talks about long backpacking trips he took as a young man, how he almost completed the Pacific Crest Trail. I'm impressed; completing even one-third of that trail is an amazing feat. He's really proud of the fact that he had a fly rod with him for his entire PCT trek. Now he owns a home with a working farm and grows fresh fruits and vegetables year-round.

I like Ziggy. He's a nice, friendly, interesting guy. On top of being a pleasant person, he's also a good fly fisherman. Watching him fish is cool—it's as if all the natural forces of the river, the fish, and his rod flow in one fluid movement of timeless art. It's as if he's experiencing everything at once. Most people mentally hop from one thing to the next—river, fish, work, bird, guide, family, fly selection, back to the fish, and so on. For Ziggy, it's different. In his misty eyes and fluid motions, I can see everything meeting in one perfectly seamless moment.

Ziggy and I catch a handful of fish, photograph some bald eagles, spot a couple moose, and even sit and watch a pod of cutthroats rising to green drakes. Most of us would jump at the chance to cast to a huge pod of rising trout, but Ziggy abstains. "It's too beautiful a thing to disrupt the flow of nature," he says.

Instead of sending a couple dry flies down the flat, Ziggy reaches into his bag and pulls out a joint. He tokes it up and goes completely zen. For what seems like an hour, we watch nose after nose come up and eat every bug in sight. In reality, it's kind of ironic. Here we are taking in this incredible, idyllic scene...while countless trout murder and terrorize helpless mayflies just a few yards away.

Later in the day, I get to know Ziggy on a whole new level when we pull up to Falls Creek Falls. It's a beautiful hundred-foot waterfall cascading over four different levels of massive river rock. A famous spot among the fly fishing community, it's been pictured on numerous fly fishing magazine covers and calendars.

As I row toward the waterfall, Ziggy takes a bunch of photos. He waves for me to pull into the eddy below; from here, we can get a better view and feel its magnitude. As I row into the back current of the waterfall, Ziggy asks me, "Is it safe for people to cliff jump off the falls?"

"Yeah," I tell him, "Happens pretty often. But only off the second level."

Now Ziggy wants to do some cliff jumping.

I pull into the slowest part of the back eddy and Ziggy begins to disrobe, removing one piece of clothing at a time until he's down to his boxers. I have my fingers crossed that those boxers stay on, but, to my dismay, they, too, hit the deck. Ziggy proceeds to bend over right in front of my face, putting on his Keen sandals. I am shocked—momentarily paralyzed, really—by the stark, sudden nudity of this man in my boat. Then he jumps into the cold, clear waters of the Snake River.

Ziggy swims toward the waterfall, gets to the edge of the rock pile and slowly starts the ascent to the first tier. He's got his Keens to protect his feet, but I can't help but think that he has forgotten to protect his greatest asset. The thought of his manhood slapping the water after a fifty-foot free fall has me preemptively wincing.

After a few minutes of climbing, Ziggy has made his way up to the second tier. There, standing tall and proud in all his glory, Ziggy pauses for a moment, then launches himself through the air toward the mighty Snake. I cringe and look away before he hits the water.

There's a huge splash, and I look over my shoulder to see Ziggy already swimming back to the rock pile. Apparently, he wants to try it again. I can't believe this guy isn't drowning from the pain of a naked, fifty-foot cliff jump. He's got some balls. Perhaps it's the weed, but Ziggy seems unphased. Clearly, this is not his first bare-ass cliff jump.

He's climbing up for a second go…and another boat comes around the corner. Cameras once pointed at the picturesque waterfall drop as friendly fishermen shake their heads in laughter at the sight of a naked, hairy, middle-aged man in Keens standing right in the middle of this natural wonder.

Could Ziggy be embarrassed?

He quickly jumps off the cliff. *Splash!* Then waves at me to row over. I rush on the oars to retrieve my needy, naked client. I get the boat close and he grabs the side, hanging in frigid snow melt until I can get out of sight of our river neighbors. Once around the corner, I help Ziggy back into the boat.

"You need some time to dry off?" I ask as he gets settled in the bow.

"I'm fine," he says. "I'll just air dry."

"So, you wanna take a short break?" I ask.

"Nah, I'll just air dry as I fish."

"What?!" I blurt out reflexively.

He repeats himself.

"Yeah, I heard you the first time," I assure him.

"Do you have a problem with that?" he asks.

"Man…the customer's always right, but—naked fishing?! I've never had a naked fisherman in my boat before," I say. "I'm not sure what to think about that."

"It's just natural, man," Ziggy replies.

"I don't care how natural it is," I tell him. "You *have* to put your pants back on."

Ziggy laughs. He leans down. Instead of his pants, he grabs another joint.

So there, three feet in front of me, stands naked Ziggy, lighting up a joint, trying to find his "happy place" in nothing but a pair of Keen sandals. Once his joint's sufficiently lit, he reaches down for his fly rod. "Let's go do some fishing," he says.

"Buddy, I like you," I reply, "But pants would go a long way to helping me get you down this river."

Ziggy smirks as he looks back at me. "Come on, Ryan, isn't this the purest of situations? Man stripped down to his bare flesh, meeting the river in the most natural of settings?"

I shake my head in disbelief as I pull up my anchor to start the most awkward hour of my entire life. My general affinity toward this man is quickly changing. I look up to begin rowing down the river and all I can see is a full moon eclipsing the sun. I pull closer to the bank and Ziggy starts ripping off line, thereby becoming the first-ever—and hopefully last—naked fisherman in my boat. He starts to cast and quickly gets into the rhythm of the river.

Within a few minutes, Ziggy has a nice trout on the end of his line. As I stand up to net the fish, I contort myself as far away from his nether parts as possible. The fish hits the net, and I notice there are way too many things swaying with the motion of the boat. I'm just hoping the fly stays put in the trout's mouth and doesn't somehow snag a sensitive part of Ziggy's anatomy.

For the next hour, I'm forced to look past Ziggy's naked form while I attempt to navigate the boat past rocks and debris. I find myself wishing for a swifter current. Eventually, mercifully, the burn of the sun reflecting off the water and onto his tender skin convinces him to put his clothes back on. Thirty minutes later, we arrive back at the launch.

Sometimes life presents us with experiences that become etched into our memories. Some of these memories we cherish. Others haunt us. And as badly as we may want to erase the troubling ones, they end up sticking as much as the ones we recall fondly. I know I will remember Ziggy the Naked Fisherman for the rest of my life. Whether I want to or not.

EYE CANDY

When you guide day after day for months on end, the trips tend to blur together since most follow the same script. However, every once in a while, routine gets tossed out the window and you have a day that puts a big old smile on your face. This story is from one of those days.

It started like any other day. I'm right on time as I pull into the lodge parking lot, grab my cooler filled with lunches, waters, sodas, and a couple beers, and place it in my boat. I see on the schedule that I'm part of a two-boat trip for three people, along with another guide named Ned.

Walking toward the fly shop to get the necessary flies and leaders for the day, I hear the morning chatter coming from the guides, mostly centered on the incredible Pale Morning Dun hatch the day before.

"Did you see how many bugs were out there yesterday?" says one.

"It seemed like every fish had its nose out, trying to sip up those mayflies," says another.

I assume the hatch is going to be huge again, so I load my plastic fly cup with different PMD imitations—patterns like the Rusty Spinner, PMD Challenged, and Sparkle Dun in sizes 16 to 18. I also grab some nymphs—a few beadless Pheasant Tails, Lightning Bugs, and Rainbow Warriors—to cover myself in case the fishing isn't quite as stellar as the day before. Each day on the river is different, and we've got to be ready for most situations. Next, I grab two nine-foot 4x leaders and a bottle of dry shake because we'll need a lot of floatant to keep those little dry flies riding high. I run through my mental checklist, decide I have everything I need for the day, and look for my clients.

It's 8:30 a.m. and half the guides have already taken off for the day, but my anglers are nowhere to be found. I pull up a chair and take a look at a two-year-old Orvis travel guide, happily dreaming about fishing in far-flung destinations. Then I remember I'm a guide and can't afford to travel to any of these places. Providing food for the family and paying the mortgage doesn't leave much extra for Giant Trevally in the Seychelles. But, like everyone tells me, I have the best job in the world— well, except for the benefits plan.

"Where the hell are these guys?" asks Ned as he walks through the door.

"Just think of this as paid relaxation," I tell him. "Hey, have you ever thought about going to Tasmania to catch the rare green-spotted brown trout with teeth like a great white shark?"

Ned laughs and gives me a look. I've always thought of him as an uncle. At the time, he was in his early 50's, but the sun had aged him a decade or more. His tan, leathery, wrinkled skin was a constant reminder to always go heavy on the sunscreen. Ned is considered one of the veteran guides on the river and has taught me a bunch over the years. He's a pleasant guy who doesn't get his feathers ruffled very often, and anyone would be lucky to spend a day in his boat.

As Ned and I talk about our dream fly-fishing destinations, the phone rings and interrupts our conversation. The receptionist at the front desk picks it up. Ned and I look to the clock and see it's now 10 o'clock.

"Glad I got up early this morning," I say. "You think these people are gonna show, or are we getting a paid day off?"

"I could go for a day off," says Ned. "This'll be my twentieth day on. My hands and back could use a rest. I'm not a young buck like you anymore."

Now Sebastian, the manager of the lodge, walks into the fly shop. In addition to managing the lodge, Sebastian has also been a guide, chef, and hotel manager over the course of his career. He is the ideal candidate for running a fly-fishing retreat. His fun-loving, friendly, larger-than-life personality is one you can't get enough of, and a conversation with him always leaves you with a smile. He's a great manager and all the guides respect him.

"Boys, I have some good and some bad news," he says "Which one do you want first?"

"Give us the bad news first," says Ned.

"The bad news is, you still have to work today," Sebastian says.

"And the good news?" Ned asks.

"The good news is, the clients won't be here until 11 o'clock," says Sebastian. "So hang in there, and I'll be back when our guests show up."

Right at 11, we hear a vehicle turn off the highway into the fly shop parking lot. Ned and I grudgingly get up from our comfortable seats to go meet our clients for the day. As we step outside, I notice a pimped-out Escalade in the parking lot.

"Huh. That's a new look," I think to myself. "Maybe Jay-Z has taken up fly fishing."

The Escalade doors open, and I see three-inch glossy black heels stepping out of the driver's door.

As the rest of the driver is revealed, I see she's wearing designer jeans and acrylic nails, her hair is styled, and she's recently been to a tanning salon. My initial assumption is that she's dropping off her husband and his buddies for their fishing trip, but she's promptly joined by two ladies who are equally dolled up. It's like three Let's Go Fishing Barbies come to life.

Ned and I walk over to introduce ourselves. The women appear to be in their early 40's, though I imagine they've been telling people it's their 37th birthday for at least half a decade. Being a young man in my late twenties, I find them attractive for middle-aged women. It's evident they care about their appearance and take care of themselves. They're invested. As we chat, they mention that they need to go into the fly shop to pay for the trip, so we head that way.

After a few awkward steps on the gravel pathway, they slip off their high heels and walk barefoot the rest of the way. "Bummer," I think to myself. "Those were going to be the perfect wading shoes."

Ned and I hang back while the ladies head to the desk. Immediately they start giggling with Sebastian, but after a minute or two their conversation turns to hushed tones and they occasionally glance over at Ned and me. Eventually, Sebastian comes over and asks us to step outside.

"Hey, guys, these ladies are looking to have a fun day on the river, and they have certain, shall we say, *expectations* of their guides," says Sebastian.

"What does that mean?" Ned asks.

"Well, they say they want guides who are 'eye candy,'" Sebastian replies.

Both Ned and I start laughing.

"So, what does this mean for us?" I ask.

"Well, Ryan, you make the cut, but they want a replacement for Ned," says Sebastian. "They said they were already married to old guys and have had enough of men over 50. They only want to fish with young, fit guides."

Danger! Danger! Danger! Cougar Sighting at the lodge... and I'm happily married.

"Well, I needed a day off anyway," says Ned with a grin, taking the news in stride. "Besides, I forgot to put the curling iron in my boat this morning." We all laugh at his joke as Ned heads to his truck.

"What's the plan now?" I ask Sebastian.

"I'm going to go call Andy to replace Ned," he says. "You go and get these ladies ready for the day. That way, when Andy shows up, you'll be rigged and ready to start fishing."

I lead the trio back to the Escalade, wondering the entire time to what degree these cougars intend to prey upon me.

"Do you ladies need rods or are you planning on using your own?"

One of them opens the back of the SUV and hands me a

rod tube. I unzip the reel compartment to reveal a purple-and-pink Abel fly reel attached to the butt section of a high-end Scott fly rod.

"Wait a minute," I think to myself. "What the heck are you doing with this?"

Out of the corner of my eye, I notice the heels exchanged for wading sandals and the designer jeans for quick-dry shorts. I'm having a hard time wrapping my head around the whole scene, but I'm starting to think maybe my first impression was way off.

I finish rigging up the first rod and I'm handed the second rod, this one with an Abel reel adorned with Yellowstone cutthroat graphics with bright yellow and orange streaks and large black dots.

"That purple-and-pink reel is for girly girls," the second woman says, needling her friend. "I'm a true fly fishing woman."

I am totally impressed. They have the right gear, they're talking some legitimate smack, and they're looking good doing it. The third rod is similar to the other two, and the reel has a matte light-green finish; she tells me it's her favorite color. After I get all three rods rigged, Andy pulls up in a frantic rush.

Andy is younger than me, barely old enough to buy alcohol. He fits the "eye candy" description perfectly—tall, thin, handsome, and strong from rowing a drift boat most days. As soon as he gets out of his truck, the Cougars pounce on him. They introduce themselves and start flirting instantly. Being single, Andy soaks up the attention with a big, boyish grin on his face.

We load the ladies and their gear into our trucks and tow our boats to the river. By the time we get to the launch, it's almost noon. The ladies hand me a cooler with Chardonnay and strawberries for an after-lunch snack, and Andy and I quickly put the boats in. Andy has one angler in his boat, while I have the other two.

I row across the river to hit the first bank and instruct my clients to get ready. As we approach the bank, they stand up, unhook their flies, and start ripping off fly line. I notice how confident they both look. The first one casts and her fly lands perfectly about six inches off the bank; the second one follows with the same result. It isn't long before we've landed several nice cutthroats on small PMD dry flies. The one with the cutthroat-colored Abel remarks happily, "These cutties are so much prettier than my reel!" I can't help but chuckle.

After about an hour of fishing, we decide it's time to stop for lunch. I pull over on a famous riffle where I know the fish will start feeding heavily on PMDs in the afternoon. Andy sees that we have pulled over and starts rowing toward us. As he approaches, I quickly realize that Andy is now guiding with his shirt off, and his client has a small sparkle of drool in the corner of her mouth. Over lunch, the ladies steadily flirt with him. He's starting to get that air about him, as if he thinks he'll be going home with at least one of them.

We learn that all three of them had divorced in the past 5 years, with each taking their successful husband for half of his net worth. Each woman owns a house on the beach in Ventura, California, and a summer home in Jackson Hole. During the summer, they fish together once a week and hire a guide once a month to take them to a different spot. These women must've been married to idiots. When you have a stunning wife who likes to fly fish, you need to protect her like she's the last specimen of her kind.

Andy and his amused admirer finish lunch and head off to fish the afternoon hatch. My clients and I stay at our lunch riffle a little while longer to see if the hatch will go off again. Sure enough, about 20 minutes later, the bugs start pouring off and the riffle turns into a feeding frenzy as every trout in the vicinity starts to rise. For an hour, the ladies take turns hooking fish after fish on small PMD dry flies.

After a while, they tell me they're bored and want me to find them some more challenging fishing. I don't think I've ever had clients like this before. These ladies are cool, fun to hang out with, want to find bigger, more challenging fish, and they're making me feel like a teenager again. So I pull up the anchor and continue our drift down the bubbling river.

Over the next hour or so, we catch a few fish off the banks, then I find another spot with countless noses trying to suck up little mayflies in the foam. The ladies are ecstatic to see rainbows in the 18- to 20-inch class rising consistently. One of them cracks open the white wine. It's not long before we land a couple big rainbows, and then the wine really starts flowing.

Not one more fly is cast for the rest of the afternoon. Refills are poured every 20 minutes, and before long, both bottles of Chardonnay are empty. The ladies have had their fill of fishing; the rest of the day is filled with laughs, awkward compliments, and fish tales.

I woke up that morning assuming I would have another routine day on the river. Then I met my clients, and my first instinct was to hop in my truck and drive away as fast as possible. But that was before I knew exactly who they were. That day turned out to be my favorite day on the river that season, and it made me rethink my perspective on first impressions.

Sometimes first impressions are accurate and reliable. But in this case, these high-heel-wearing fisherwomen had a side to them we couldn't see.

Andy didn't hook up that night, but I can tell you this: those Cougars are still prowling around the lodge every season looking for fresh prey. And hey, maybe when the Cougars become Sabertooths, Ned will finally get his shot too.

DRY OR DIE

Let's be honest: When it comes to trout fishing, everyone loves throwing dry flies. There's something magical about tempting a fish to leave its lair, to rise to an imitation insect made of feathers, or rare snow leopard fur, or a clump of hair from your own pet, in a pinch.

All fly tyers have tried to tie the perfect dry. The thought of being that tyer, The One Who Created a Masterpiece, the one that will fool the wiliest of trout gets us excited.

Dry fly fishing is much sexier than fishing an indicator (or "bobber," if you're from the Deep South) with split shot and multiple flies. It's not as exhausting as throwing streamers, and it doesn't require the precision of swinging emergers at a precise depth during the middle of a hatch.

Instead, you can cast a dry fly effortlessly, watch it fall gently to the water, add the perfect mend, and, if everything goes right, a fish instantly appears from the depths. A spot that seconds before looked like nothing more than water flowing over rocks suddenly contains life! The fish moves, and the sun lights it up, brilliant shades of gold, green, brown, yellow, and pink. The colors flash before your eyes as the fish slowly rises. Will it eat, or merely inspect? This time, the fish isn't a taker. Something about your fly was a little off, and you take note to use chocolate Lab hair rather than golden retriever with your next tie.

I love to fish dry flies. In fact, for the first six years of my fly-fishing life, I never once threw an indicator or even a streamer—it was dries or nothing for me. Learning to fly fish during the summertime on the smaller rivers of western Wyoming, there was never a reason to do anything else. If the fish didn't eat the dry, the dropper nymph below would surely catch it.

However, once I was introduced to nymphing and streamer fishing, I quickly gained an appreciation for other areas of the sport. Today, my favorite method of trout fishing is ripping streamers on the banks of big Western rivers. Target shooting with a heavy streamer and searching every hole and rock on the bank is like weaving a motorcycle through a traffic jam.

Cast, strip, strip.

Go around the next rock.

Pause, let it drop.

Strip, strip, strip.

Accelerate the cast.

Hit the spot.

Strip, strip.

Wham!

The line goes tight and instantly you feel a throbbing head shake! It's a thrill unlike any other in fly fishing. And even so, fishing dries reigns supreme for many anglers. For them, it's literally "dry or die." One day on the river I guided just such an angler.

It was an overcast day with dark skies. Given the weather conditions, I knew it would be great for throwing large stone-fly dries on the bank. The PMD fishing wouldn't be stellar; the browns and cutties would be looking for larger bites. The streamer fisherman in me wanted to cast heavy-weighted Wooly Buggers against the bank to see if we could find the big one, but having left my hard hat at home, the last thing I wanted was a size-2 tungsten-beaded Wooly Bugger bouncing off my skull at Mach 1.

I quickly put the streamer terrors out of my head and returned to thinking about large dries on the bank, like a purple Chubby Chernobyl. That's right: a *purple* Chubby Chernobyl. On highly pressured rivers like the South Fork of the Snake in Idaho, fish sometimes get used to the standard colors of tan, yellow, and brown. Oftentimes, the same fly tied in red, purple, or pink will be the hot ticket. With the dark conditions and lots of people on the water, I decided to go with the purple Chubby. (I highly discourage a blue Chubby, but that, my friends, is for another story.)

When I got to the shop, I met Charles, a nice, solemn man in his 60's who looked like he'd just walked out of an Orvis catalog. He was dressed in a white short-sleeved guide shirt tucked neatly into tan khakis; a nice brown leather belt; brown loafers; and an olive-colored, wide-brimmed wool hat. The hat, with its sheepskin band loaded with dry flies, quickly caught my attention. The fly collection included everything from small mayfly patterns to large attractors. If that hat could talk, I'm sure it would tell stories of fishing small creeks in England and limestone rivers on the East Coast, sight-casting to large browns in New Zealand and hooking fat cutthroats on large Western tailwaters. His hat was quite the accessory, and it perfectly complemented his fishing attire. Charles and I quickly started up a conversation about the day.

"I'm really excited about the overcast conditions," I told him. "I think these clouds are really gonna get the big fish hungry. It should be a great day for fishing dries."

Charles listened intently. As we chatted, we wandered around the fly shop, gathering up a collection of stone fly patterns and making sure to grab a few extra purple Chubbys.

"We probably don't need any of these flies," I teased him. "I'm sure the years' worth of flies on your hat could get us through the day."

He laughed at the comment. "Yeah, there are some good flies on this old hat of mine. They've caught lots of fish," he said. "Sometimes I just grab my rod, reel, and a fresh leader and go out to see how many fish I can catch on the flies that live on this green hat."

How awesome is that? More anglers need to adopt Charles' perspective and forget about buying every fly in the shop. Overloaded sling packs tend to be the norm these days, but most anglers only fish a handful of dry fly patterns in a variety of sizes. The Parachute Adams, Royal Wulff, Elk Hair Caddis, and Stimulator tend to be the bugs we reach for first. That size-26 Rusty Spinner you bought to fish the San Juan doesn't see a lot of use. Ninety percent of the time, all the flies you need are on Charles' hat.

Before long, another guide, Blake, walks over. Blake had

taken Charles out the year before, and Charles' hat had caught his attention from across the room. Blake is a really nice guy and a great fisherman. He's well-respected in the guide community and has guided for many years. Blake is probably best known for his sense of humor and playing practical jokes on other guides.

"Charles! It's good to see you again," said Blake. "Hey, I wanted to add a fly to your collection. I've been saving it in my fly box out in my truck. Can you guys hang on a minute? I'll be right back."

As the guide turned to leave, Charles flashed a small smile. I could tell he was appreciative and touched by the gesture. After a couple minutes, Blake returned, with an awkward smirk on his face. He reached in his pocket and pulled out a round plastic fly cup containing a single fly. Blake carefully handed it to Charles who took it and held it out so the three of us could all examine the masterpiece.

At first glance, it appeared to be a standard size-12 purple Parachute Adams, a fly the guides at the shop call the Purple Haze. As I looked at it more closely, though, I noticed something peculiar about the fly. The upright post in the middle of the fly was tied with a brown, wiry material. Charles also noticed the odd-looking strands and asked what they were.

"It's a type of rare African monkey hair that floats amazingly well," said the guide. "With that monkey hair tied in the middle, it'll float higher than the Titanic before the iceberg."

As Charles inspected the fly further, Blake gave me a quick wink. Charles took off his hat and found a spot amongst the ageless ties near the front of the sheepskin band. He thanked the other guide and shook his hand.

"I'll go pay for these flies and be right back," Charles said to me.

After he walked away, I turned to Blake. "Hey, man, I know you didn't tie that with some rare African monkey hair. What is it?" I asked discreetly.

"Can you keep a secret?" he asked.

"Of course," I said.

"I cut off a handful of my pubes to tie into that fly," he said under his breath. "I was wondering if I could get the Pubic Fly, now known as the Brown Mop, onto Charles's famous hat. Mission accomplished."

I shook my head and tried to stifle my own laughter as Blake cackled to himself the whole way out of the fly shop.

Charles strolled back up. "You ready for some fishing?"

"Absolutely," I said. As we walked toward the exit, I couldn't take my eyes off the Brown Mop, swaying in the breeze of the overhead fan.

Charles and I hopped into my old SUV. We had about a 20-minute ride to the river, so we started up some nice conversation. After a while, Charles pivoted his body toward me.

"Ryan, we need to talk about the fishing today," he said.

"Okay. What do you have in mind?" I asked.

"I only want to fish for the rise," he said after a couple moments.

"That's fine. You'll be fishing dry flies the whole day," I said, nodding. "I had no intentions of nymphing or throwing streamers. If you're a 'dry-or-die' kind of fly fisherman, then that's great."

Charles shook his head. "I don't think you understand what I mean."

"You're talking about fishing dry flies, right?" I asked.

"Well, yes. But I don't want to hook any fish today," he said.

I glanced over at Charles with a puzzled look on my face. "What do you mean 'not hook any fish'? Isn't hooking fish the goal?" I asked.

"Yes, for most people," Charles said. "But I'm not your average fisherman. You see, I've fished all over the world. I've caught thousands upon thousands of fish in my lifetime. I no longer have a desire to hook fish. For me, the joy of fishing now is fooling the fish and getting them to rise to the fly. I know what a 22-inch cutthroat feels like. I've tugged on an 8-pound rainbow. The excitement for me is all about tricking those trout to eat dry flies like that Purple Haze Blake gave me."

I nodded my head as if I understood, but I couldn't believe the words that were coming out of Charles' mouth.

"Okay, this is a new one for me," I said. "So, I guess you want me to cut off your hook point and then guide you like I would for any other trip?"

"Exactly," Charles said. "I want to fish hard and have a blunt hook point the entire time. The blunt point will be enough that I can feel the fish for a few seconds without hurting them too much. You see, I still get the pleasure of knowing that I would most likely catch the fish, but I don't have to spend any time actually fighting the fish."

"All right," I told Charles. "If that's what you want, I can make it happen."

As I rigged up Charles' rod with a purple Chubby, we talked about other trips he'd had on the South Fork of the Snake River. There was no doubt that Charles was a veteran fly angler and had experienced a lot of situations, but I was still dumbfounded when I cut off his hook point. Despite what he had said, I assumed he might "fish the rise" for a handful of fish but eventually ask me for a fly with a good hook point.

As I pushed the boat off the bank, Charles stood up in the bow, pulled some line off his reel and proceeded to paint a casting masterpiece with his rod, displaying impeccable timing and accuracy. I was taken by the beautiful symbiosis of the river, the angler, and his cast, all three in synchronicity when the fly landed gracefully upon the water. Then, poetically rising from a grassy bank, a rainbow gently slurped his purple Chubby.

Charles quickly set the hook. The rod went tight for half a second before the fly pulled through the willing lips of the rainbow. Charles then turned to me with a big smile, like a kid who just received his first bike.

"That was awesome. Great job, Ryan! Let's get another one."

I shook my head in disbelief at what I was seeing. A few minutes later it was a cutty slowly rising to the large stonefly pattern. Then it was an aggressive cuttbow. For about an hour, Charles rose a half-dozen fish, and each time his passion and excitement was as high as if he had fought the fish all the way to the net.

A little before lunch, Charles made the impossible cast, the kind that wraps your fly around a rock and piles a bunch of slack that lets the fly sit in the pocket just for a second. As the fly was settling in and finding its happy place on the bubbling foam couch, an explosion occurred. Out of the water came a nose about six inches long to suck in his fly—a huge brown trout drawn to the purple Chubby like a moth to a porchlight. As the fish's head went back under the water, it caused a splash two feet in the air. *Wham!* Charles swung perfectly and drilled the hook into that big jaw. Just for a second the fish turned sideways and the sun revealed brilliant splashes of brown and yellow. Then, the 30-inch trout shook its head and dislodged the hookless Chubby from its mouth.

"That was amazing!" Charles exclaimed. "Did you see the size of that fish? It looked like a New Zealand brown! I'm pretty sure that was the largest fish I've ever hooked on this river!"

I think I'm in shock. I slowly take a deep breath. "Yep," I say. "And that was the largest fish I've ever had a client hook on this river..."

Deep down, my soul was screaming in frustration. I needed a pity party. Of course the monster brown trout I've been fishing for my entire life rises to a fly with no hook point. *On purpose.* Somebody wake me from this nightmare.

I looked up and saw Charles overwhelmed with excitement and joy, completely lost in the moment. Charles knew that was a special fish and that he could have caught it, but he had conquered so many fish in his lifetime, he no longer needed to show dominance over them. I selfishly wanted a photo with that big brown. But I realized this sport isn't about catching the biggest fish. It's about finding a balance between the fish, the river, and the angler, and trying to use a little fly to bring them all together in perfect harmony.

"I know this purple Chubby has been working for us all morning," Charles said, "but I want to try that Purple Haze with the rare African monkey hair."

"We can do that," I replied. "But do you mind tying that fly on yourself while I row us downriver for a few minutes?"

"No problem," Charles said as he reached up and unhooked the Brown Mop from his hat. After tying it to his line, he proceeded to methodically massage floatant into the hair fibers, making sure to give each a good coating so the fly would ride nice and high on the water.

"This African monkey material is awfully familiar feeling," he said. "It's definitely some weird stuff."

I nodded my head in agreement. Yep. Definitely weird.

"All right, Charles, let's see what this monkey fly has in store for us," I said. "Cast it over there on the foam bank and see if anyone's home."

The fly landed exactly where it was supposed to, a nose came out of the water, and just like that, the Brown Mop officially joined Charles' arsenal.

SABOTAGE

(A Guides Perspective to Fishing Trips)

When we go on a fishing trip, why do so many of us sabotage it with irresponsible behavior, lack of preparation, and unrealistic expectations?

In the weeks leading up to a trip, we spend countless hours dreaming about every stage of the adventure, buying all the latest gear, drooling over hours of YouTube videos, and doing so much research that we fall asleep staring at blog reports on our computer screens.

We might as well have a fishing advent calendar with teensy chocolate trouts that we eat every morning as we chase down the days to our next big trip. Rather than running to Mom and tugging on her pant leg to tell her there's only 23 more days to Fishmas, we send goofy texts to our crazy fishing buddies to remind them there's only 552 more hours until we leave. Then, the friend responds with, *I'm so excited that I tied*

15 dozen flies last night. Half of them look like crap, but I'm sure some fish will eat them. #turdfly #551morehours

There's nothing better than getting ready for, and dreaming about, the next adventure. For me, building up the excitement and anticipation of a trip is half the fun. What makes me scratch my head, though, is why we boo-by-trap our trip once we get there. Why do we expend all this energy and excitement, then not give our best effort on the water?

Well, for one, it's hard to stay that amped up for a long period of time. It takes physical discipline and mental capacity to stay on top of our game. After years of traveling with friends and guiding clients who themselves are on Fishmas Vacation, I have some insight on ways to make your next fishing trip more successful.

What's the first thing most of us do when we finally arrive at a fishing destination with our friends? We open a bottle or head to the bar and let loose on the first night of the trip. We are excited. We're ready to celebrate. We're on a fishing trip with our best buddies—finally! It totally makes sense to want to get liquored up on that first night. I have to admit, there's nowhere else I would rather be right now than sitting around a table with my best buds, drinking, talking fishing, and dreaming about the next day on the water. Just the thought is like a shot of whiskey that warms my heart.

For most of us, after a couple too many drinks, the voice of responsibility starts to break through. We look at our watches and say, "Crap, I have to be up in 4 hours to get on the water. Well, boys, it's time for me to hit the sack." As we head to bed, we know we had a ton of fun and it'll be a night to remember for a long time. What we don't think about is how it'll affect our fishing skills the next morning.

I often wonder why we go big on the first night, before we ever wet a line. Why don't we save all those drinks for the last night to celebrate another great trip? We should postpone the big hurrah for when our fishing skills and clear minds are no longer needed. Somehow, though, the bottle tempts us like a beautiful woman at the end of the bar.

Maybe it's because we're all conservationists at heart. Somewhere deep down, we know we need to give the fish a fighting chance, so we buy another round the night before. Who cares how many missed opportunities we're creating? It's not like we were gonna keep the fish anyway. #ijustbrokeoffanotherfish #imabetterfishermanthanthis #whendidiforgethowtocast #isuckatflyfishing #hungover

The next morning, the alarm clock goes off early, and we struggle to lift our heads from the pillow. It's Fishmas morning! But we feel more like the Mom and Dad now, up all night making everything perfect for everybody, setting out milk and flies for the magical Fish Claus, hoping he'll bring us gifts of rising trout, rolling tarpon, schools of bonefish, and blitzing stripers. Yet the kids come limping out of their rooms with aching heads and gurgling stomachs. (No, that's not a gurgler fly deep inside of you.) Somehow, we all manage to get to that first and second cup of coffee and get our butts to the water, but once we're finally on the river, all we can think about is going back to bed.

Wait, what?

Dreaming about this day for months, now all we want to do is go back to bed? What's happening here? What happened to all of that energy and excitement? Oh yeah, we lost it at the bottom of that bottle last night.

After years of guiding and taking fishing trips myself, I've learned that if you want to get the most out of your trip, it's best to wait and have the big drinking night on the final evening. That way, when you wake up on the first morning, you are one-hundred-percent on your game. When you get that one grab from a big chrome steelhead, you'll be less likely to miss it. When you have to make a 60-foot cast into the wind to a huge tarpon, you might actually get it done. When that pod of trout is sipping tricos early in the morning, you might not put the whole pod down with your hungover casting. Being semi-responsible on the first night will greatly enhance your fishing trip. Plus, by the second night, your buddies will be so tired from fishing all day, the chance of drinking too much is greatly reduced.

With that said, you definitely have to make sure you have some fun. Surely fishing trips are not all about the fishing; hanging out with friends is just as much a part of the story afterward as the tales of fish caught and missed. Learning how to manage the drinking on the first night will help you to be a better angler throughout the trip. Know what your limits are and stick to them. If you want your own YouTube moment, you have to be somewhat coherent to see the fish, make the cast, set the hook, play the fish, and bring it to the net.

Of course, to have a completely successful YouTube moment, you also have to be able to cast your fly rod with some level of proficiency. Generally speaking, most anglers think they're better casters than they actually are. Somehow, we spend so much time mentally preparing for a trip, but we miss the most important part of the planning process: We never actually practice our casting. We get to the destination without having made a cast since our last trip. That's not a big deal if your last trip was six to eight weeks ago. However, if your last trip was six to eight *months* ago, you'll probably be rusty—and that's putting it nicely.

If you're going to do one thing before your trip, practice casting. Then, if you can handle a second thing before your trip, practice casting. And if you can manage to squeeze a third thing before your trip, purchase a lesson from a casting instructor. I can't stress enough how important it is to have sound fly-casting skills. Your cast is the start of the whole process, and if you are not proficient, you need to invest the time to make yourself a more qualified angler. And, if you become a really good caster, it might even help you overcome a hangover! That doesn't mean you'll enjoy the process, but at least the fish will be hurting right along with you.

The last big tip: have realistic expectations. We spend a lot of time fantasizing about the trip, and when we actually get there, we're confronted with the reality that it's still "fishing." We're inclined to think that every trip will be epic and the fishing conditions will be perfect. Most anglers usually don't have real expectations of what will happen on the water. The reality is, most of the time, the fishing is average and the weather normal. For a lot of anglers, "average" fishing is great, but competitive anglers want the best all the time. Somehow, in the midst of our pre-trip fantasizing, we have to figure out how to let go of those idealistic thoughts and try to get into a "thankful" mindframe instead.

The thankful mindframe involves being happy that we're

on an amazing trip with our friends, that we have the financial resources and physical ability to make the trip. It goes a long way to having a positive attitude. We need to be thankful that we live in a country—and on a planet—so full of natural resources that we will never be able to experience all the beautiful watersheds in one lifetime. Being thankful while fishing enables an angler to take in the whole picture of what's going on all around. The fish, the scenery, the sounds, the smiles of friends, and the feeling of a bent rod all fold into the mix of the trip. If you can get into this kind of mindframe, everything will slow down, and you'll be able to fully enjoy the trip you spent so many hours dreaming about.

This mindset will not only make your fishing experience more enjoyable, it will allow you to better reflect on it later. Six months after your trip, assuming you didn't drink yourself to smithereens, you'll be able to sit back and sip a cocktail with fond memories of the entire experience. The reason we all take these adventures is so we can anticipate the excitement beforehand, experience the thrill during the trip itself, and forever relive the memories that were created with our friends.

There's nothing better than a great trip. Just make sure you exhibit a little responsibility, practice your casting ahead of time, and come with the right expectations. Then, somewhere in the midst of all of that, find your inner child and be glad that another Fishmas morning has finally come.

WHEN NATURE CALLS

E ach day I hit the water, I have no idea what will happen with the clients, the weather, or the fish, but 99 percent of the time the day goes just like the one before it. I wake up early, meet my clients, catch some fish, have a couple laughs, head home to the family, and prepare to do it all over again the next morning.

Then there are the days I fish with new clients who forever live in my fish story memory bank. One such day in Idaho, I was supposed to take out a client from the Lodge at Palisades Creek named Martha. Martha was one of the Lodge's longest-standing clients, but her usual guide was booked with other anglers for the day. I had met Martha at the Lodge previously and found her to be a sweet and upbeat woman. At the age of 72, she wasn't going to let anything stop her from a day on the river. Martha loved to fish and knew the ins and outs of the sport. She grew up fishing with her father and brothers and had a passion for fly fishing.

Martha's husband Bruce, on the other hand, was not an outdoorsman. But she dragged him along nonetheless. Bruce would have preferred to be in a big city enjoying the opera, but he knew that Martha loved to fly fish, so he became a fly fisherman, too.

I knew that there were some expectations of me that day. I had been entrusted with a great client of the Lodge, and since I wasn't their regular guide, I needed to show Martha and Bruce an especially good time. After chatting a few minutes in the fly shop and purchasing the necessary gear for the day, I walked out the door. Another guide pulled me aside.

"You're gonna have a great time today," he said. "Martha's a lot of fun to guide, but there's a coupla things that might surprise you. Don't worry about it, but she is one rugged woman."

As I walked away, I pondered what he had told me. What could be so surprising about Martha? Was it her fishing ability? Her personality? Something physical? I convinced myself that I had seen almost everything by that point in my guiding career and brushed off the thought. I was about 27 years old at the time, so I was extremely optimistic, and wrong.

The three of us headed down to the river, chatting about their experiences at the Lodge and how things have changed over the years. In the 30-minute drive to the river, I decided this would be an easy day. They didn't want a long, hard day; at this point in their lives, they were just excited to catch a handful of trout. I started thinking about my own life, how I was getting a preview of what it would be like to have my bride beside me in our golden years, catching a few trout on dry flies.

Martha and Bruce have figured something out. Their mutual respect and love for each other stretches beyond the normalcy of life, and they support each other in their dreams. Martha's dream is to fly fish; Bruce's dream is to be immersed in the arts. I wondered how two different worlds could collide and then work so well together. What a beautiful portrait of how opposites attract and how 50 years of a loving marriage and friendship can result.

We took our time at the boat launch. Once the rods were rigged up with large foam dry flies, we started our float. It didn't take long to see that Martha was quite proficient with a fly rod for a woman of her age. She must have been one hell of an angler in her younger days. The years may have diminished her reaction time, but she wasn't going to let that discourage her.

"I may not be a good nymph fisherman, but my old, slow reflexes are perfect for dry fly fishing," she said matter-of-factly. I laughed and nodded my head in approval. I was just impressed she could still get the fly reasonably close to the bank.

Now, Bruce was another story. It was clear he was just along for the ride. He would take long breaks and only fish when Martha started catching a few. He liked being there in the outdoors, enjoying the scenery and taking in the wildlife. He kept asking me about Broadway shows, operas, ballets, and museums, some of which I had seen and visited, as I too have an appreciation for the arts. However, my level of knowledge on the matter is fairly shallow, and I was unable to keep up with Bruce as he talked about underlying themes of Shakespeare. Just about the moment he started to go deep, Martha yelled in a frustrated voice, "Bruce! This is my vacation! I don't wanna hear another word about Shakespeare! For goodness' sake, shut up and fish. Ryan, tell me a funny fishing story." I once again laughed at her sharpness and then dove into the fish story memory bank.

After a couple hours of fishing, Martha and Bruce had caught several trout and were having a pleasant day of fly fishing. I got to a spot in the river where there are a series of side channels flowing off the main stem and decided to take one small side channel with several good riffles that are typically full of cutthroats feeding on pale morning duns. As we started down, Martha piped up from her seat in the bow.

"Ryan, nature is starting to call, and I need to pee."

"No problem," I said. "Let me pull over at the bottom of this side channel and we'll find an easy spot for you to get out."

I rowed downriver for a couple of minutes, pulled off to the side, and dropped my anchor on the bank.

"Do you need my help getting out of the boat or walking across the rocks?"

"Well, Ryan, usually I don't get out of the boat," she said. "I've had two hip replacements over the last five years and these legs of mine are not good on uneven ground."

"Oh! Okay," I said. "So, how do we go about you answering the call?"

"Well, usually I slide my butt off the side and just go from the boat," she replied casually.

Now I'm realizing what the other guide was talking about. I could picture him and the other guys back at the Lodge laughing their asses off knowing what was about to happen in my boat.

"Okay," I said. "Whatever you need to do, go for it."

"Ryan, you need to turn around and promise not to look," Martha replied.

I laughed and shook my head at the person who would try to sneak a peek of a 70-year-old woman's butt. That was not me.

"You don't have anything to worry about," I told her.

Frankly, the sounds I heard painted a perfectly vivid picture. The unsnapping of the button on her jeans. The zipper ticking down. The pants hitting the deck. Then the boat leaned to the left under the weight of her body and the unmistakable sound of pee hitting water filled the air. I had never witnessed a woman urinating off the side of a boat before, but it seemed she was quite the pro.

Suddenly I heard the sound of muffled voices. Sure enough, another guide boat was heading down the side channel at the same time Martha was relieving herself. I thought to myself, "You better speed it up, Martha," just as the boat appeared from around the corner. Now the voices were as clear as day.

"Oh my God. Is that a woman peeing off the side?"

"Wow, that is not a pretty sight."

"I wasn't expecting to see that on the river."

The next thing I heard was Martha giggling.

The other guide boat passed us as my boat rocked back and forth with Martha getting put back together. "Ryan, you can turn around again," she said. "Those boys just got the show of their lives!"

Instantly, Bruce, Martha, and I started laughing hysterically at the awkward, funny, and precarious situation we had just experienced.

The rest of the day went as I expected. Fish were caught, stories were told, laughs were had. But nothing would come close to the show Martha had put on in that side channel. She made me realize that at her age, the small things in life don't

RYAN JOHNSTON

matter. Sometimes you're in a situation you can't control, and you just have to roll with it. So what if someone sees you taking a leak—as long as it's not a police officer who could write you a ticket for indecent exposure.

Situations like Martha's can be embarrassing or they can be handled with grace and laughter. Martha got that one right and never thought twice about it. After all, everyone pees, and when nature calls, there's no ignoring it. When we find ourselves in an embarrassing situation, we can remember Martha, and laugh it off with our friends.

STEAMY WEATHER

When it comes to weather, you can encounter all kinds of things on the river. Thunderstorms, heat waves, cold spells, rain, snow...the list goes on. Of course, you can experience a wide variety of weather conditions pretty much anywhere, but when you're in the great outdoors, the weather dictates where you can go and what you must wear, and it can make things miserable for the unprepared. Case in point: One particular day when my clients were not prepared for the steamy conditions we encountered.

It was already 90 degrees in Swan Valley that morning, and the temperature was expected to rise above 100 in the afternoon. For people from the Deep South or Desert Southwest, this is just a walk in the park. But for people from Idaho, we thought that hell was getting a little too close to Earth. I've experienced quite a bit of heat, but when it's 100 degrees at

6,000 feet elevation, it feels like the sun is trying to give you third-degree burns. There's not enough sunscreen in the bottle to protect you from that.

My clients that day were two brothers from Vermont named Bruce and Petey. When I met them in the lodge, Bruce was in full waders, boots, fleece jacket, and beanie. In addition to his waders, Petey wore a hoodie and a ball cap. My first thought was, "If they don't take those waders off immediately, they will have some nasty, sweaty conditions going on inside of them." As we discussed the day, I mentioned that it would be over 100 degrees that afternoon. Bruce and Petey looked at each other.

"I thought it was cold in the Rockies?" Petey replied with surprise.

"Well, yeah, at certain times of the year it can be really cold, but in the summer, it's usually nice," I told them. "We've been having a heat wave for the last week and it's been much warmer than usual. So, I suggest you take off those waders and cold-weather gear."

Bruce and Petey heeded my advice and went back to their cabins to change their clothes. They returned 30 minutes later wearing blue jeans and long-sleeved technical fishing shirts. It was an improvement over what they showed up wearing the first time, but still not appropriate for the expected conditions. I decided to roll with it and let them experience the Rockies as they had envisioned.

Within the first hour on the river, it became evident that it was a sweltering day. I was rowing the boat in my normal guide outfit—shorts, light technical fishing shirt, flip flops, and ball cap—and I was already sweating my ass off. It was one of those days when you get a thick sweat band around the brim of your baseball cap and salt crystals build up on your skin, all just while sitting still. We were pounding bottles of water every 20 minutes and it was like the fluid was flowing out of my skin at the same rate I was consuming it.

It didn't take long before Bruce and Petey's long-sleeve shirts started sticking to every part of their chests and backs. Their pit stains stretched from their elbows to their chests. Even with the hot weather, Bruce and Petey were hanging in there and fishing hard. Both were experienced fly casters, yet somehow they had missed the boat on common-sense apparel. We floated down the river all morning, throwing dry flies toward the banks, and by lunchtime we had landed a handful of fish.

As each hour of the day went by, those jeans looked less and less appealing. By two o'clock, Petey was making comments like, "It is *really* getting hot out here" and "I'm definitely wearing the wrong clothes."

Meanwhile, I was fighting the stinging sweat running down my forehead into my eyes. This is a constant battle that guides in hot weather must deal with. If it's not sweat getting in your eyes, it's the sunscreen. I was guiding with one eye open, thinking things like, "Where did his fly go?" and "Was that a fish that just ate his fly?" and "How come I can see his fly with one eye but he can't see it with two?" And also, "I hate sunscreen."

Another hour had passed when Petey asked, "Is there a place where we can cool off for a bit?"

"You want me to find some shade?" I asked.

"I would love to get out of these sticky clothes and go for a swim," Petey said.

I rowed downriver for another 10 minutes to find Petey a nice, slow, deep, blue pool to take a dip in. What happened next is something I will remember until the day my friends and family lower me into the ground.

I pulled over to the side of the river and told Petey it was safe to jump in.

"Man, this is going to feel good," Petey said, smiling back at me.

First he peels off his sweat-soaked shirt. Now I'm wondering if he'll swim in his jeans or if I'll be exposed to some unwanted manhood.

I promptly got my answer.

Petey unzips his jeans and shimmies out of them. He rolls his jeans down to reveal…*a royal blue man thong*.

At my first sight of this tiny, V-shaped piece of "underwear," I couldn't stop myself from laughing out loud. Then, Petey proceeded to bend over, his hairy white ass right in front of me. My initial laugh turned into hysterical, nonstop howling. Bruce joined me.

Petey wrangled his feet out of his sweat-soaked jeans and turned around with a confused look on his face.

"What's so funny?" he asked.

I looked up at him with a grin on my face. "What are you wearing that for?" I asked.

"Oh, this little thing?" said Petey.

"No, the socks," I said sarcastically and laughed some more. "Yes, that little thing!"

Petey looked down and adjusted his manhood as if showing off. He then looked back up at Bruce and me.

"My wife finds it sexy," he said proudly.

I glanced around.

"I don't see your wife in this boat," I cracked.

Bruce burst into laughter. Now the two of us were giggling like two high school girls that had just seen the varsity quarterback in his boxers. Bruce and I started throwing around remarks like, "I guess I know who wears the panties in that relationship."

Petey eventually went for his swim, a glistening white ass bobbing up and down as he made laps in the calm pool. I can't say for certain, but I am 90 percent sure I heard the river start to cry as Petey entered the water. After the cooling swim, he got back in the boat, dried off, and put his clothes back on.

"That felt great, but I'm not sure how much good it did. This is one steamy afternoon."

"Is that how your wife describes your g-string?" I asked.

Petey chuckled. "Let's do some more fishing."

As we took off down the river, I could still hear it moaning from pure disgust. Needless to say, the rest of the day got warmer and warmer. The fishing was average. It wasn't a great day, but it wasn't slow either. Fish were caught and released as thoughts of a man's ass in a blue thong kept attacking my brain.

By the end of the day, I was so sweaty, I looked like a dog that had just climbed out of a pool. It ended up being one of the warmest and funniest days I ever experienced in the Rockies. One thing I know for sure: Simms or Patagonia could make a collection of quick-dry thongs for my friend Petey.

Who knew Petey would be the most prepared of us all? I wish I could have guided in my underwear. Then again, when I think about the sheer amount of places I would've had to apply sunscreen, I suppose wet, sticky clothes was the better option. I just wish Petey had kept his pants on because visions of Big Blue still haunt my nightmares.

THE SIXTH SENSE

My first experience with a fly-fishing guide was the first time I held a fly rod. At the age of twelve, a guide in Idaho taught me the basics in fly casting and fishing. And since then, I've been fortunate to fish with guides all over North America. From the freshwater rivers of the West, to the blue water of southern California, to the flats of Florida, I'm lucky to have been guided by lots of amazing and interesting people. Every guide is unique in his or her personality, style and demeanor. Each one with their tan, leathery skin, calloused hands, and tired, crinkled eyes has a story about how they became a fishing guide. I love hearing these stories.

Like the executive who grew tired of the professional world and found peace and connection with the water. Or the fish bum who lives in his van down by the river and takes people fishing to pay the gas bill for his next adventure. Or, like me, the kid who could never get enough of fishing and ended up making a profession out of it. There's even one famous guide who, at one time, was the head football coach for a major Division I college before he got tired of the coaching lifestyle and became a flats guide instead. Every guide story is rooted in one basic idea: There may be way more money in the professional world, but you can't beat the joy, passion, and peace that's found on the water.

I once hired a guide who had given his entire life to the sport. From a young age he immersed himself in casting, fly tying, and learning the intricacies of the mighty Rio Grande River. He spent a lifetime learning every pocket, rock, and drop-off where a willing trout would live. He loved every aspect of the sport and loved sharing his passion with other anglers. To this day, of all the guides I've had the pleasure of fishing with, he is the most interesting one I've ever met. That one evening I fished with him still leaves me in awe today.

I was on a fishing road trip with my best childhood friend Mike—we were making our way down the western side of Colorado at the ripe young age of 19. We had planned an epic two-week fly fishing trip starting in the northwest corner of the state and ending up on the Rio Grande in southern Colorado. Along the way, we had hired guides on the famous tailwaters of the Fryingpan and Taylor Rivers, but we were most intrigued by the Rio Grande.

We had called the local fly shop to hire a guide for an evening of dry fly fishing. The fly shop connected us with one of their local guides and instructed us to meet him at the shop at 5pm. Eager to hit the hatch that night, we arrived 15 minutes early and were welcomed by the owner of the store, Ben.

Ben was incredibly warm and friendly as he talked to us about the river, the fish of the Rio Grande, and what to expect during the evening hatch. Like most fly shop owners, he walked us around the shop making sure we had enough flies, leaders, and tippet. After a short while, Ben wanted to chat about our guide.

"The gentleman you guys have tonight has been guiding this river longer than anyone. His name is Charles. Charles has spent his entire life in this valley learning everything there is to know about the trout of the Rio Grande. He knows this river like the back of his hand," Ben said.

"Sounds great. Thanks for connecting us. We're looking forward to it," I replied.

"Well, boys, there's more to Charles' story than just being a great fishing guide. You see, Charles is probably unlike any other fishing guide you've ever hired," Ben said.

At this point, my friend and I were starting to wonder what all of this meant. Mike and I took a quick glance at each other with puzzled looks on our faces.

"Okay, well, tell us what we need to know," I said.

Ben looked down to fidget with papers on the counter. Then he looked up with a regretful look on his face.

"See, the truth is, Charles is legally blind," he said.

"What do you mean, legally blind?" I blurted out. "Like, he can't see? Like, no vision at all?"

Ben nodded his head. "Yep, that is correct."

"How does someone guide with no vision?" I asked, incredulously. "How does Charles know where he's going? How does he wade in the river? How does he tie flies on?"

"I know this is a surprise and a different situation than you guys were expecting," Ben said.

"Yeah, you think?" Mike said sarcastically.

"Ben, we paid a lot of money for this trip, for a great experience on the river. We've never been here before–having a blind guide seems like the start of a disastrous trip," I said.

"I know, I know…" Ben said. "Trust me, I've heard every possible question about Charles being a blind fishing guide. You guys need to trust me on this one. Charles is a great guide and person. You will absolutely love your trip with him."

Mike and I both shook our heads in disbelief.

"I don't see how this trip goes well," I said. "I know a lot about fly fishing, and if you don't have your sight, you are seriously limited in your ability to be successful on the water. A person's eyesight is the most important physical sense they have to help them navigate the water and fishing."

Ben put up his hands as if to stop all the questions and comments.

"Boys, I know that you have serious doubts about Charles and his guiding abilities, but trust me when I say he knows this river better than anyone. If you have a bad experience with him, I will refund your money after your trip. I know you will have a great experience and will not be disappointed," Ben said.

I look over at Mike once more for consensus. "Okay, if you're gonna put a free trip on the line, we will give Charles a chance," I conceded.

Just as those words left my mouth, the front door opened and an older man, shuffling his feet and tapping a white cane in front of him, entered the shop. *Tap, tap, tap*, went the cane as he made his way to the counter, successfully avoiding a display of Scott, Winston, and Sage fly rods.

Charles was a gentleman in his mid 60's. He wore khaki

shorts and a faded light blue guide shirt. His hair was gray, his full beard was untrimmed, and his skin was tan and leathery. He looked a bit like a man who couldn't see himself in the mirror.

"Charles, good to see you, my friend," said Ben. "Wow, you're looking very spry and spunky today."

Charles laughed. "You should have seen how fast I ran our local marathon last week. I was blazing by those younger folk," he joked.

"Come here, old man, and give me a hug," Ben said with a smile.

Ben walked toward Charles, put his hands out to reveal his position, and they embraced like it had been years since their last meeting.

"Charles, I would like you to meet your two clients for the day, Mike and Ryan," Ben said. "These two young men are excited to fish with you and to learn about some dry fly fishing on our beloved Rio Grande."

Charles put his arm out and started moving it around to find us. I gently touched his arm and gave him a firm handshake.

"Nice to meet you, Charles," I said.

"Likewise," Charles replied. "Do you guys need rods? Have you bought all the hot new flies Ben has tried to sell you? Do you have enough dry fly floatant?"

"Yep, we have everything we need," Mike said. "We didn't buy all the hot flies, but we should have enough to get us through the evening."

"Good. I'm glad you didn't waste all your money. Half of those flies are better at catching fishermen than fish," Charles said. "I have some secret patterns I tied myself here in my pocket. They will work just fine."

Charles started ruffling through his pocket and pulled out a fly cup with a half-dozen Parachute Adams.

"*Those* are the secret flies?" I asked.

"Yep, the secret Parachute Adams," Charles said. "No one knows about this fly. Whatever you do, don't let Ben see it."

Everyone laughed at Charles' sense of humor.

"Well, guys, I need to let the cat out of the bag," he said. "In case you didn't notice, I'm blind."

"You don't say," Mike cracked.

Charles got a good chuckle out of Mike's sarcasm. "This evening there should be a great mayfly hatch," he said. "I'll need you guys to drive me to the river and help me walk down the bank. Once we get to the water, I'll take it from there and show you some incredible spots on the beautiful Rio Grande."

Mike and I were still in disbelief that we were talking to a blind fly-fishing guide. After a few more minutes of chatting, we helped Charles get to our truck.

Charles loaded into the front passenger seat and started giving us directions to his favorite spots.

"Ryan, go ahead and drive to the stop sign at the end of town," Charles said. "At that stop sign, you'll turn left. Then you're gonna drive for 10.7 miles and there will be a dirt road on the right."

I drove to the stop sign and turned left as instructed, then started watching my odometer closely.

After about 10 mins of driving, Charles spoke up again. "Ryan, you're getting really close. Do you see that dirt road coming up on the right?"

I peered a half-mile down the road and, sure enough, there was a dirt entrance that looked like the start of a road.

"Yep, I see it," I said gratefully.

"Okay, good. Turn right on that road and that will take us to the river."

Within minutes we had arrived at the beautiful freestone river bubbling its way down to the Gulf of Mexico. I parked the truck and Mike and I helped Charles out of the front seat.

"Alright, guys, we made it," Charles said. "Hand me your rod tubes and I'll get your rods put together."

We assured him we could rig our rods ourselves.

"No, no. The job of a guide is to help his clients. Let me see those things," Charles said.

Not wanting to offend Charles, Mike and I reluctantly handed him our rods.

Charles slowly and methodically took the rods out of their tubes and put them together piece by piece. As he looked off into space, he peeled line off the reels and ran it through the guides, careful not to miss a single one. He unraveled fresh leaders and tied them onto the end of each fly line. Then he reached into his pocket, pulled out the secret Parachute Adams flies, and tied one on.

Mike and I looked at each other in amazement.

"Charles, that is impressive," I said. "How did you do that without your sight? I can barely do that with 20/20 vision."

"Let's just say I've had lots and lots of practice," Charles said. "After fly fishing for the last 60 years, I can rig a rod up in my sleep. To be honest, I used to make more mistakes when I had my full vision. Now I just slowly feel my way up the rod, making sure to hit every guide. Tying knots is easy—my hands can feel everything that your eyes show you.

"Alright, boys. Can you help me down the trail to the river?"

Mike and I each took an arm and slowly guided Charles down the trail. After a 20-minute snail's pace walk, we got to the water's edge. Mike and I were still wondering how our blind guide was going to help us catch any fish.

"Ryan, do you see that riffle right in front of us?" Charles asked.

"Yes…"

"Great. Now, take your fly and cast it right next to that big rock at the top of the riffle. Can you see that big rock? Can you see how there's a soft seam coming off the left side of the rock?"

"Yes, I see exactly what you're talking about."

I proceeded to wade into the river and cast at the target set by my blind guide.

I made a good cast and the fly gently landed to the left of the rock. Instantly, a nose came out of the water and sipped in my Parachute Adams.

"Get him! Set the hook!" Charles yelled.

I quickly lifted my rod and firmly set the hook in the trout's mouth, coming tight to a beautiful 21-inch rainbow that cartwheeled its way across the river. My reel sang as Charles laughed.

"That's an awesome fish!" Charles said excitedly. "Mike, get the net. I want you to net Ryan's fish."

Mike ran over to the bank and grabbed the net. He quickly entered the water below me and scooped up my first Rio Grande rainbow trout. I walked over to Charles and gave him a pat on the back.

"Thanks for that, Charles," I said, catching my breath. "That was a great fish and fight. But, how did you know the fish ate my fly? You couldn't see it, and it didn't make any noise."

"Well, you know, Ryan, I've been guiding this river longer

than you have been alive, and I have developed a sixth fishing sense after years and years of feeling the river's energy," Charles said with a stern look on his face. "I can feel an energy change in the water when a fish eats a fly. It's almost like how Yoda uses the force to move things. I use the 'Guide Force' to feel the energy of the fish and the water."

"No way. Really?!" I asked, incredulous.

"No bullshit. That is the absolute truth," Charles said.

Mike and I looked at each other in wonderment.

"Huh, I guess you must be some kind of Fish Whisperer," I said.

Charles then began to laugh loudly.

"Ha-ha! I got you guys with that one," Charles laughed. "I'm a blind fishing guide. I can't feel no freaking energy. That rainbow you just caught has lived behind that rock for the last five years. I've had clients catch that fish hundreds of times. He's like my own pet trout. I call him Ricky the Rainbow."

Mike and I both laughed at how gullible we had been as we patted Charles on the shoulder.

"Come on, guys. Guide me to the next riffle," Charles said. "This time we'll let Mike fish for Betty the Brown."

Mike and I spent the next four hours helping our blind fly-fishing guide around the river. Charles showed us numerous nooks and crannies he had memorized over the last 60 years. He proved to us that a guide's memory and mastery of the river is just as important as being able to see everything.

We never asked Ben for our money back. We both left smiling at the end of the day, having had an experience we would never forget. It was a once-in-a-lifetime evening with a great friend, a great hatch, and a great fly fishing guide.

THE DARKEST OF NIGHTS

It was almost my 21st birthday, and my two high school fishing buddies and I decided that we would spend a week fly fishing in southwestern Montana for the occasion. Every summer since graduating high school, we had headed to the Rockies with fly rods in hand, and each year we chose a new spot for our fishing adventures. It was a time of growing up, each of us in search of ourselves and a deeper meaning to life. On these trips, we saw amazing parts of our country, one of us fell in love, we all smoked our first cigars, and we had our first tastes of alcohol. These trips were the pinnacle of the year. Every dollar and penny earned was saved to fund these week-long treks of adventure and freedom.

In previous years, we had fished the San Juan, Frying-pan, Taylor, and Green Rivers. None of us had ever fished in Montana before, so we decided to head to Dillon to try our luck on the famous Beaverhead, Big Hole, and Ruby Rivers. My friends Michael and Sam left our hometown of San Diego one hot August afternoon and drove to northern California to pick me up from my college apartment in Davis.

They got to my place late that evening and immediately crashed on the living room floor after the long drive. The next morning, I woke to a beeping alarm at 4 o'clock, walked over to my pals still sound asleep in their sleeping bags, and gave them a gentle nudge. Michael quickly popped up and put on his clothes, but waking Sam is no easy feat. If he's in a deep sleep, there ain't much that can stir this hibernating bear. Ten minutes later, still serenaded by Sam's deep, vibrating snore, we did what any desperate fishing buddy would do: bombed him with pillow blows to the face.

Eventually Sam came to. Being on a college life, shoe-string budget, our plan was to drive the 15 hours to Dillon in one day to avoid having to pay for a hotel. By 4:30am, we were in my truck, drift boat in tow, headed down the interstate, pumped to be on our third consecutive summer-time fishing road trip. Our excitement was at a whole new level since we finally had a drift boat to fish out of, and the craft would make its maiden journey on this trip. The radio blared as the sun began to rise, and in that moment, we were untouchable—three young guys on the open road with the air of freedom filling our lungs.

We had no way of knowing that before the trip was over, we'd collectively endure one of the most terrifying experiences of our lives.

We watched the sun rise and set that day, dazzling us with yellows, oranges, pinks, and purples. For hours in between we talked about life, girls, and, of course, fish. Once again, we were all together. The "Three Fishing Amigos" had been reunited, and we hadn't missed a beat. The truck seemed to drive itself as each hour floated by. Before we knew it, we rolled into the quaint little city of Dillon.

Dillon is one of the Rockies' many fly fishing hubs. It sits quiet and still in the winter and quickly becomes a bustling town of drift boats, fly fishermen, and outdoor enthusiasts in the summer and fall. It was nearly dark when we pulled into the gas station to fill up, each of us groaning and stretching as we extricated ourselves from the truck. Staggering to the pump and the bathrooms, we knew we still had a long night ahead of us setting up camp on the banks of the Big Hole River. My truck and boat were loaded down with camping equipment. We drove about 20 minutes outside of town to find an old gravel frontage road that headed down to the river.

The clock hit 10 o'clock as we pulled into the campground. We set up the bare necessities by the light of a lantern, pulled the food cooler out of the truck, and unrolled our sleeping bags to get a good night's sleep. Even though we'd had a long day of travel, the thought of fishing the next day had us tossing and turning all night long. Every hour on the hour I looked at my watch in anticipation of the adventure.

As the sun began to rise, the inside of the tent took on a blue glow as the rays pierced the nylon fabric. I unzipped my sleeping bag, letting in the brisk Montana air. My two counterparts were still lost in their dreams of chasing girls and fish. I poked my head outside to see the mighty Big Hole River only twenty feet away. Standing there in nothing but my boxers and shoes, I took in the majesty of the moment before the kiss of the air taught me that mornings in Montana can be damned cold, even in August.

I quickly slid back into the tent and started digging through my bag, reminiscent of Mary Poppins, stuffed with clothes, waders, fly boxes, leaders, and useless gadgets, in search of something to wear. Mike rolled over, wiped the sleep from his eyes, and asked what time it was.

"It's 7am," I told him. "Time you got your sleepy ass outta bed."

Sam, the hibernating bear, covered his head with his pillow.

"Stop talking! I'm trying to sleep," he moaned.

"C'mon, man. We didn't drive to Montana to sleep," I told him, gently kicking him in the ass.

After a quick breakfast, the three of us headed down the road to fish the famous Beaverhead River. We stopped at the local fly shop to get the latest fishing report and figure out what flies we'd need for the day. The guy at the shop suggested that we use small midges in the morning, as most of the hatches were going to come off later in the day. After buying a handful of zebra and WD-40 midges, we were back in the truck on our way to the river.

We decided to check out a local spot and spend the morning wading. Upon arriving at the river, we were introduced to a very small, intimate watershed with crystal clear water and olive, black, and brown creatures swimming around and feeding voraciously. Every few moments a trout would rise from the dancing grass growing on the bottom of the river and open its white mouth to inhale another snack. We stood on the banks of the Beaverhead, mesmerized by the sheer quantity and size of the trout below us.

We raced to the back of my truck and quickly started doing our own "Hokey Pokey," turning ourselves about with the wader-and-boot dance. Then we grabbed our rods and tied on indicator rigs with those small nymphs we had purchased at the shop.

I was the first to get my rod together and carefully scurried down the hill to the river. After walking, sliding on my ass, and hitting my knee on an extremely hard rock, I eventually made it to the water's edge. I took a big, deep breath and filled my lungs with that clean Montana air, feeling assured that all the time, money, and energy had been worth it.

As my flies and indicator hit the water, I was filled with anticipation. I threw a huge mend at the flies and my indicator settled nicely into the flat current seam. For the next fifteen seconds, that indicator moved freely as it bobbed and swirled in the current. I watched for even the smallest movement, ready to set the hook. Everything looked perfect as it floated through the slot with all the fish, yet, incredibly, nothing happened. So, I made another cast.

Then another.

And another.

Same result every time.

Shocked I didn't get a bite, I thought maybe I needed to get my flies deeper, so I lengthened my leader and added some split shot. I made another cast with a fresh level of anticipation.

Nothing.

Second cast...nothing.

I decided to switch flies. The first cast looked perfect. Nothing. Same deal on the second cast.

Now I was starting to get frustrated. I could see numerous

trout in the river, feeding frequently, but something was wrong with my flies. Could it be me and my technique? Not a chance.

I convinced myself that the guy at the fly shop had ripped us off. I could picture him laughing his ass off knowing that he had sent some touristy, young California fly fishermen to the river with midges when the trout wanted something completely different.

I reached into my vest and pulled out my nymph box, filled to the brim with flies I had acquired all over the West. Most of them I never used; they were purchased to fish a specific river at a specific time. I placed the flies from Dillon into the last openings. More flies that didn't work.

I looked through my box, trying to match the hatch, and opted for my go-to size 18 Flashback Pheasant Tail, which I trailed with a size 20 red Disco Midge. I cast my rig upriver and started a fresh drift. The indicator started to settle softly on the seam line when suddenly it jerked to the right. I quickly pulled back on the rod and felt the strong pulse of a brown trout on the end of my line making throbbing head shakes and darting back and forth through the current. Flashes of silver and yellow shimmered through the water revealing a sizeable trout.

After several minutes of fighting the fish up and down through the pool, it finally began to tire. As I started to lift the trout toward my net, it took off for the depths in one last effort to free the fly from its mouth.

Finally, the brown gave up, and I scooped it up in exhilaration. I had been rewarded with a beautiful 21-inch brown trout that ate my favorite nymph. I quickly unhooked the fish, gently supported its belly, pointed its nose into the current, and watched the amazing specimen descend to its original lying spot.

Over the next several hours, I hooked and landed many more rainbows and browns, each of them special in their own way, and each displaying God's majestic pallet—vibrant reds, pinks, greens, yellows, and oranges adorning the sides of each fish.

After a while, I began to wonder where my friends were, so I walked up the hill to find the other two amigos. At the top of the hill, I could see them fishing different riffles downstream of me. I walked down and watched them for a few minutes, both completely immersed in their environment. Determined. Committed. Their casts were precise, every movement fluid and effortless.

After a few minutes, they noticed me standing on the hill and reeled up to come meet me. We talked about fish missed and landed and agreed it was a great call to come to the Beaverhead on the first day of our trip.

A short lunch break, and we were back on the river, flogging the water with our casts. We covered miles of river as we plied every nook and cranny in search of that elusive monster brown trout.

By the end of the day, we were beat. We had fished since mid-morning and now the sun was starting to set. A full day of fishing will really wear a person out, and by the time we got out of our waders and back into the truck, we thought it best to grab dinner in Dillon. When we finally arrived back at camp, we found ourselves completely swallowed up by darkness. No moon, no streetlights, no house lights—just utter, eerie darkness. The first order of business was to get the fire started.

As Mike got the campfire lit, Sam and I opened a couple

beers and toasted a great first day of fishing. It wasn't long before the fire was raging and the three of us were completely relaxed in our chairs, staring into the fire and talking aimlessly about the fishing and what the plan would be for the next day. We agreed to fish the Big Hole right in front of camp.

After several more beers, the fire started to lose its energy as the flames slowly diminished. With just a few flames flickering back and forth amidst the hot coals, the blackness once again began to intrude. Then, as we finished off the last of our beers, we heard a branch snap on the other side of the river. The three of us quickly looked up.

"Did you guys hear that?" I asked.

Both Mike and Sam nodded their heads while staring out into the darkness.

"Maybe it was a deer or moose moving around," I said. "Or maybe it was just a dead branch falling off a tree."

Sam, being a hunter for most of his life, looked at me and said, "I don't know what that was, but it probably wasn't a deer or moose. Those kinds of animals bed down for the night. And it definitely wasn't a branch falling. It sounded like something being stepped on."

"Do you think someone is over there watching us?" Mike asked.

"Okay, let's not scare ourselves here," I said. "It could be a person, but it's more likely an animal. If it is an animal, and we ruled out a deer or a moose, then the only other option is a bear."

"If it's a bear, we need to take some preventative action here," warned Sam. "Mike, build the fire up again. Ryan, take the cooler and put it back in the truck. I'll go get a big flashlight and see if I can spot something on the other side of the river. If it is a person, then we should find something to protect ourselves with. Everybody grab a knife just in case."

The three of us scurried around camp trying to do exactly as Sam told us. A bear or some crazy lunatic out in the woods surely warranted some precautions. However, as we stared out into the black wall of darkness across the river, there were no more sounds. In a matter of minutes, we had the fire raging, the cooler locked up, our knives in our pockets, and our flashlights in our hands. We tried to peer out across the river, but the light from our flashlights barely reached the other side. We scanned the bank looking for any sign of life–a squirrel, a deer, a person, Sasquatch. None of us could see or hear anything out of the ordinary.

After what felt like hours, but probably only five minutes by the clock, we gave up and settled back into our chairs. We dared not talk, our senses heightened as we listened for whatever could be out there. The fire cracked and stirred as the wind started to blow through the trees. Time passed slowly, allowing our once rigid bodies to become relaxed again. We started joking about what could have been out there. After 30 minutes of nothing, we agreed it was probably just some animal passing by on the opposite side of the river, and when the fire went out, we would go to sleep.

As the fire started to fade for a second time, the three of us sat quietly, putting off going to bed. Suddenly, another large branch snapped on the other side of the river, seemingly 10 times louder than the first time. We quickly sat up in our chairs, looked at each other and tried to peer out into the darkest of nights.

"There is definitely something over there," Mike said.

"Yeah, but what?" I replied.

"It's almost like something is stalking us," Sam said, officially freaking us out. "Only when the light is low does the thing move."

Just as he said that, this "something" hit the river at full sprint. As the bounding creature splashed its way through the water, the three of us leapt to our feet and simultaneously yelled, "Run!"

We sprinted as fast as we could for my truck on the other side of camp. With each step, all we could hear was massive amounts of water being displaced by something big and fast heading straight for us. As we dashed toward the truck, Sam ran into me and knocked me to the ground.

"Open the truck! Open the truck! C'mon man, hit the lock!" Mike and Sam yelled as I rolled around on the ground, trying to pull my keys from my pocket.

I got to my feet and hit the remote to unlock the doors. I reached for the front door, but Mike threw it open first, jumped into my spot and quickly slammed the door shut. I stretched for the back door handle, opened it and jumped in. Once inside, Sam hit the lock button and all three of us lunged toward the windshield, peering out into the pitch-black night.

"Turn on the headlights so we can have a better view of camp," I told Mike.

Moments later a big grizzly walked into our camp, snarling and showing its large, sharp teeth. Its claws dug into the soft dirt as if searching for something to tear apart. The bear walked directly in front of the truck and stared at us through the windshield. We looked at each other in horror and then back at the devilish bear. It snarled again and then let out a screeching roar that pierced our souls. Just looking at him, we knew he wanted to eat us. He had spent hours stalking us, waiting for the blackness of night to hide his approach.

Mike honked the horn at the powerful bear, trying to get it to run off, but the terrible beast was unphased. It slowly investigated the vehicle, sniffing it with its big, wet nostrils. We were frozen. Shocked.

After making a lap around us, the bear turned its attention to the rest of our camp, snooping and sniffing, looking for something to eat. Then, in an instant, he got to the edge of the headlights' beams and disappeared into the darkness.

"Now what?" I asked.

"Well, I'm not sleeping out there anymore," Mike said.

"Me neither," Sam agreed.

"Okay, then, what should we do?" I asked again.

"Let's just sleep in the truck," Sam suggested.

"No way in heck I'm sleeping in a truck with you guys all night!" I responded. "Let's drive back to Dillon; I'll get the three of us a hotel room."

I switched spots with Mike and drove us toward town. While we talked about how amazing and scary the encounter was, I hit a raccoon as it was trying to cross the road. A racoon. I hit a raccoon.

Then, not much further down the road, I hit a deer. A deer. It was running down a steep hill and continued right into the highway. The deer smashed solidly into my door–I could see the terror in its eyes the moment before its life ended. I connected with that harmless animal, knowing that just minutes before, I had been in the same position. When the bear was trying to take *my* life.

After thousands of dollars of damage to my truck, but still driveable, we made it to Dillion. We found a hotel and the three of us were able to get a decent night's sleep without any bears hunting us down. And nothing else was killed.

The next morning we went back to camp and packed everything up as fast as we could. All around camp, we saw footprints of the beast who had run us off the night before. These were the paws that had tried to make us its dinner. The prints were bigger than two of our feet put together, and the claw marks were as long as large knives.

We all decided that we had experienced enough of Wild Montana for one trip and decided to go to Idaho instead for the rest of our fishing vacation. We had a great time making memories in Montana, but camping was never the same after that one dark night.

THE FINAL CHAPTER

Rarely in life do you get to experience something truly inspirational—a moment that is deeply impactful, beautiful, and life-changing. I'm talking real life, not a scene in a movie. These moments don't happen very often, but when they do, they stay with us forever. Moments like your wedding day, the birth of a child, landing the job of your dreams, or the passing of a loved one.

I can honestly say, I've only had *one* of these deeply inspirational events ever happen while on the water fly fishing. It was the kind of day that left a group of friends smiling, laughing, and crying all at the same time.

This story is about my good friend Jim. Jim was a great guy–a special guy. Raised with a fly rod in his hand, he was taught how to fish on the small creeks of Northern California by his father, Steve.

Over the years, Jim would grow into an accomplished fly fisher and eventually became obsessed with steelhead fishing. Who could blame him? Steelhead are one of the most transcendent freshwater fish to catch. The steelhead's power, speed, erratic movements, and jumping abilities make them an incredibly special species.

In Jim's twenties, he landed a beautiful wife, Emily, and together they had two beautiful "hen" daughters and one handsome "buck" son. A great husband and father, he loved his family well, and they loved him.

The unrelenting call of fly fishing and steelhead always brought Jim back to the river. The river was a place of peace for him. It was a place where he found healing, time for reflection, and time for prayer. The cold running waters revitalized him and gave him a deeper connection to the world, himself, and God. This deeper connection would ultimately lead Jim to a calling as one of the pastors at my church.

Jim was an awesome pastor. He was an encourager, willing to jump in and support people any way he could. Over the years, he brought people together through fly fishing, eventually creating a fishing group within our church. Jim brought all of these men together for fellowship and bonding through the water and fly fishing. The river became Jim's sanctuary, his place of ministry. He wanted to create connection through fly fishing by having deep, meaningful conversations, observing God's creation, and simply sharing a beer with his friends.

I was lucky enough to become one of Jim's favorite fly fishing guides. I got to observe firsthand the relationships he created through the sport. Jim would frequently hire me as a guide and invite a friend in need of encouragement. Year after year, I had the honor of being a small part of Jim's ministry. When Jim came out on the boat, there was greater purpose than just fishing. Yes, we always had a good time and fished hard, but there were bigger things happening. The guided trip wasn't about the fishing; it was the vehicle through which he would positively impact someone's life.

When Jim hit his late thirties, he was diagnosed with colon cancer. It was a shock, and a battle that Jim fought, off and on, for eight years. He went through multiple rounds of chemotherapy, but with the cancer spreading throughout his body, it was a steep battle. One day, after his third round of chemo, Jim was in the boat and not feeling great.

"Jim, why do you keep going through chemo when you know you can't beat this thing?" I asked him.

"I do it for my kids," he said. "Anything I can do to have one more day with my kids is worth it. Even if I have to feel crappy and my body's broke down, it's worth it to be able to drive my kids to school one more morning."

As time passed, Jim's cancer continued to spread and have a greater effect on his body. In the last year of his life, he set a goal to catch a coastal steelhead—the pinnacle of the steelhead fishing world. Catching a steelhead mere hours or even a couple days after it's left the ocean is completely different than catching one hundreds of miles inland. Coastal steelhead fishing is highly addictive. The fish routinely cartwheel across the river and quickly pull large amounts of backing from reels. These fish are so powerful and fast that I have seen three different reel drags completely explode as they dared to handle the fish's might. In my opinion, the coastal steelhead is the king of freshwater fish in North America.

Jim was an avid steelhead fisherman but had yet to land a coastal steelhead. So he and a group of friends planned a five-day trip to go catch Jim his prized fish. They drove up to Southern Oregon to fish the famous steelhead waters of the Chetco, Elk, and Sixes Rivers. Sadly, Jim became very ill on the first day of the trip, and the group had to return home before even hitting the water.

Jim became so obsessed with the thought of the coastal steelhead that he even got one tattooed on his forearm. This tattoo ran along the inside of his arm from his elbow to his wrist—it was an amazing interpretation of a steelhead, and his daily reminder that he had yet to achieve his goal. A month after his cancelled Oregon trip, Jim called me and asked if I would take him and his best friend, Anthony, to the California coast for another shot at catching a coastal steelhead. We set a date for early March on the Eel River, situated deep in the Redwoods.

Five days before our trip to the Eel, Jim called me to say he wasn't feeling up for making the long drive. We chatted for a few minutes, and I asked if he and Anthony would like to do an easy half-day trip on the Lower Sacramento River instead. Jim said he would like that, and asked if he could bring his wife Emily along, too. I agreed that having both his wife and his best friend on the river for the day sounded like a sweet time, so we set a plan to meet at the boat launch the following weekend.

On the day of our float, I showed up at the river early and got the drift boat and rods all prepped. I had the boat in the water when they pulled up in Jim's truck, with Jim in the passenger seat and Anthony driving.

As soon as Jim saw me, he smiled and waved. I was a little

taken aback at the sight of him. I hadn't seen Jim for two months, but it was obvious the cancer had really taken a toll. He had an oxygen tube in his nostrils, had lost tons of weight, his cheeks were sunken in, and his skin had a light gray tint to it.

Anthony hopped out of the truck and gave me a big hug.

"Jim can't walk anymore," he told me. "What's the best way to get him in the boat?"

"Drive down the boat ramp, and we'll do an easy transfer from the truck to the front seat of the boat," I told him.

Anthony got back in the truck and drove down to the water's edge. I pulled the drift boat up to the edge of the concrete to create a safe place for everyone to step. Then, Anthony and Emily worked together to get Jim into the boat.

"Where's a good place to put the oxygen tanks?" Anthony asked.

"I've never had oxygen tanks in the boat," I said, "but we can pull the cooler out and make extra space."

With everyone onboard, we pushed off and headed downstream. Jim and Emily sat next to each other in the front. Anthony was in the back of the boat and I sat in the middle, rowing. A little ways down the river, Jim turned to look at me.

"Man, I'm glad to be here. Thank you for doing this," he said. "It's good to be alive."

I smiled back at him and nodded my head in agreement. As I looked at Jim, I wondered how many days he had left. I wondered if he would be able to hold the rod, let alone cast. Only time would tell what Jim could still do.

My plan was to get to one riffle where lots of fish had recently been caught. As we approached it, I told Jim and Anthony to get ready to start casting on the left side of the boat. Anthony stood up in the back. Jim slowly shuffled his feet to turn his swivel seat to the left. He grabbed a rod and pulled off some fly line to begin his cast, lifting up his arm and lobbing an indicator off the side of the boat. It wasn't pretty, but it was good enough to catch a Lower Sac rainbow.

Jim threw a mend and studied his indicator intently. Within seconds of his tandem fly rig hitting the water, Jim got a violent strike that pulled the indicator several feet below the surface. He tried his best to set the hook but didn't have the physical strength to respond quickly enough. His head fell to his chest in disappointment as he knew he'd just missed a solid grab.

"Don't worry about it, my friend," I told him. "Get the next one."

Jim nodded his head and lobbed another cast into the riffle. Within a minute he got another strike, and just like the time before, his reaction was too weak and slow to set the hook. I patted him on the shoulder.

"Keep swinging. You'll get 'em."

At the end of the run, I back-rowed to the top of the riffle to give Jim and Anthony another try. The second pass resulted in Anthony hooking and landing his first rainbow of the day. Jim got another chance, but sadly missed that one, too.

The third pass down the run had the same result, with Anthony landing a beautiful fish and Jim missing his opportunity.

Same story on the fourth pass. Now I was starting to doubt that Jim still had the strength left to hook and land a fish.

But on the fifth pass, everything came together.

Jim made another awkward cast, and within seconds his indicator went down so hard that it almost jerked the rod out of his hand. Jim slowly lifted the rod tip up in the air and got just enough tension to hook the fish. Out of the water jumped a beautiful 21 inch rainbow. It wasn't the big, chrome coastal steelhead that Jim had dreamed of, but the fish put a big smile on his face, nonetheless.

Jim fought the fish for a long time as he struggled to hold the rod up, but eventually brought it to the net. The four of us marveled at the beautiful rainbow with a striking crimson-and-pink stripe down its side. We took a couple pictures and let the fish swim back to its home in the riffle.

Jim looked at me and smiled. "That was awesome. Thank you so much," he said. Then he sighed. "I don't think I could do that again. But Emily has never caught a fish on a fly rod. Would you be willing to teach her how to do it? Then I can take a break and watch her fish."

I happily agreed and pulled off to the side of the river so I could teach Emily the basics of fly fishing. After about twenty minutes of practice casting and setting the hook, we continued our way downriver.

It took a little while before Emily got comfortable with the casting and mending. Before long, though, she got her first strike, and the indicator shot under the water. She missed the hookset.

Second take, same result.

On the third strike, she set her hook fast enough, but the fish jumped out of the water and threw the hook.

The fourth fish broke her line.

The fifth fish came off as well.

Jim was her biggest fan with each one, gazing adoringly.

We got to the final riffle of the day. Emily cast her line, and we slowly drifted along without a bite.

I rowed back up to give the riffle another try. Again, nothing.

I back-rowed up the run a third time, and Emily cast again. We passed through all the best water with no result.

Suddenly, in the tailout of the run, Emily's indicator rocketed under the water, and she quickly set the hook. The line came tight, and the battle was on! She did everything perfectly and *landed the fish*–with the boat launch in sight.

Joyous celebration ensued.

What happened next is the most beautiful thing I have ever seen on the water. As I rowed to the takeout, I noticed Emily and Jim sharing an amazingly deep connection. It was an ending to a real-life love story as they sat there smiling and gazing deeply into each other's eyes. Embraces and kisses, love and tenderness flowed freely between them.

I realized that Jim had probably caught the last fish of his life on the same day that Emily had caught her first.

Anthony and I sat quietly, taking in the scene. Our smiles slowly grew to joyous laughter bubbling over as we experienced so much happiness from this beautiful moment. Jim and Emily turned toward us, both smiling. Then the four of us together giggled and hugged for the next few minutes.

It was as though time stood still. There was nothing else happening in the world. Just four friends in a drift boat, feeling all the joy and sorrow this life has to offer.

Jim would pass away the next morning.

I often think of that day on the Lower Sac, all the beauty God allowed me to take in. I feel honored that I was the last person to take my good friend Jim fishing. He never did catch the "gray ghost" of the coast. I wish I could have made that happen for him.

Instead, I take his best friend Anthony over to the coast on an annual pursuit of hot, wild steelhead. Anthony has become quite the steelhead fisherman over the years. Every time we fish in the coastal redwoods we reminisce about our friend Jim. We know he's in Heaven, smiling down on us. He's watching Anthony land steelhead in real life, steelhead that were only a part of Jim's dreams.

RYAN JOHNSTON

A REEL JOB

RYAN JOHNSTON

Made in the USA
Middletown, DE
05 November 2023

41719975R00104